Elise Köhler-Davidson

Spitze in Englisch
Grammatik
8. Schuljahr

MANZ VERLAG

Das Werk und seine Teile sind urheberrechtlich geschützt. Jede Nutzung in anderen als den gesetzlich zugelassenen Fällen bedarf der vorherigen schriftlichen Einwilligung des Verlages. Hinweis zu § 52a UrhG: Weder das Werk noch seine Teile dürfen ohne eine solche Einwilligung eingescannt und in ein Netzwerk gestellt werden. Dies gilt auch für Intranets von Schulen und sonstigen Bildungseinrichtungen.

Manz Verlag
© Klett Lerntraining GmbH, Stuttgart 2009
Alle Rechte vorbehalten
Lektorat: Andreas Hoffmann, Bayreuth
Herstellung: Yellowhand, Köngen
Umschlagkonzept: KünkelLopka, Heidelberg
Umschlagfoto: Fotostudio Maurer, Bamberg
Druck: Finidr s.r.o., Český Těšín

ISBN: 978-3-7863-2096-8

www.manz-verlag.de

Tipps zum Training mit diesem Buch

Dieses Buch ist genau richtig für dich, wenn du in englischer Grammatik ein wenig den Anschluss verpasst hast oder **ausführlich üben** willst, um deine **Kenntnisse zu verbessern**. Klar gegliederte Erklärungen mit zahlreichen Beispielen sowie viele abwechslungsreiche Übungen helfen dir dein Ziel zu erreichen.

Jedes Kapitel ist in sich abgeschlossen und kann von dir **nach Bedarf** bearbeitet werden. Die Auswahl der Themen und der verwendete Wortschatz orientieren sich an den **Anforderungen der Bildungsstandards** für das achtjährige Gymnasium und an den **aktuellen Schulbüchern** – es ist also **genau das, was du im Unterricht brauchst**.

Das kann ich hier üben! — Jedes Kapitel bietet dir zum Einstieg einen **Überblick** darüber, welches Thema du jeweils üben kannst.

Das ist wichtig! — Im Anschluss zeigen dir **Erklärungen mit einprägsamen Beispielen**, was du für die Lösung der Übungen brauchst.

Merke — Regeln, die du dir gut merken solltest, sind in **Merkkästen** besonders hervorgehoben.

Übung / Übung — Zu allen Themen gibt es **zahlreiche Aufgaben**, mit denen du das jeweilige Thema intensiv üben kannst. Die roten Übungen sind besonders knifflig. Wenn du diese Aufgaben ohne Fehler löst, musst du dich vor keiner Klassenarbeit mehr fürchten.

Das kann ich jetzt! — Am Ende jedes Kapitel kannst du dann für dich **selbst überprüfen und einschätzen**, wie gut du den Stoff beherrschst.

Zu allen Übungen gibt es am Ende ausführliche Lösungen. So kannst du dich mit diesem Buch **selbstständig auf Klassenarbeiten oder Tests vorbereiten**.

Inhalt

Das *simple present* und das *present progressive* 6
Zukünftiges im Englischen ausdrücken 10
Das *simple past* und das *past progressive* 14
Das *simple past* und das *present perfect* verglichen 18
Das *present perfect progressive* 22
Das *present perfect simple* und das *present perfect progressive* verglichen 26
Das *past perfect simple* und das *past perfect progressive* verglichen 30
Modale Hilfsverben mit dem Infinitiv Präsens und dem Infinitiv Perfekt 34
Bedingungssätze vom Typ I, II und III 38
Alle Zeitformen auf einen Blick 48
Das Gerundium *(gerund)* 56
Der Infinitiv 68
Gerundium oder Infinitiv? 80
Die indirekte Rede 90
Das Passiv 104
Nomen/*nouns* 120
Der bestimmte und der unbestimmte Artikel 128
Notwendige und nicht notwendige Relativsätze 138
Adjektive und Adverbien 148
Anhang: Weitere Ausdrücke und Verbindungen, die das *gerund* erfordern 156
Lösungen 158

Das *simple present* und das *present progressive*

> **Das kann ich hier üben!**   Das kann ich jetzt!
> - ❏ Wie du beide Zeitformen bildest
> - ❏ Wann du welche Zeitform verwendest
> - ❏ Mit welchen Verben du in der Regel nur die einfache Form, nicht aber die Verlaufsform verwendest

Bildung
Das ist wichtig!

Diese Formen musst du gut beherrschen:		
	simple present	**present progressive**
Aussage:	*I do, he does*	*am/are/is doing*
Verneinung:	*I don't do, he doesn't do*	*'m not/aren't/isn't doing*
Frage:	*do/does … do?*	*am/are/is … doing?*

Verwendung beider Zeitformen
Das ist wichtig!

Mit dem *simple present* und dem *present progressive* berichtest du über **Handlungen**, die **in der Gegenwart** oder **in der Zukunft** liegen.	
Verwende das *simple present* (*I do*), wenn etwas	Und das *present progressive* (*I am doing*), wenn etwas
1 **immer** so ist.	**nur in diesem Moment** geschieht.
2 **regelmäßig** geschieht.	**zu diesem Zeitpunkt** oder **um ihn herum gerade** geschieht.
3 zu einem **Fahrplan** oder einem **Programm** gehört – häufig mit Verben wie *arrive, leave, start, finish, end, open, close*.	für die Zukunft bereits **fest geplant** oder **vereinbart** wurde, meist mit Zeitangabe (einmalige zukünftige Vereinbarung).
Signalwörter: *I do* **every** day, **every** week/month/year in the mornings/afternoons/evenings at night, at the weekend**s** on Monday**s**/Tuesday**s** … always, sometimes, usually, normally, often, never, …	**Signalwörter:** *I am doing* **today, this** week/month/year **this** morning/afternoon/evening tonight, at the weekend on Monday/Tuesday … (right) now, just, at the moment; Look! Listen! It's Saturday morning …

Verwendung beider Zeitformen

> **!Merke**
> 1 **Regelmäßige/dauerhafte** Handlungen → *simple present.*
> 2 **Gerade ablaufende/einmalige** Handlungen → *present progressive.*

Übung 1

Put the verb into the correct form, simple present or present progressive.

Jack (to be) _____ very lazy. He (never/to walk) _____ anywhere. His mother (always/to drive) _____ him to school in the mornings and at 4 o'clock, when school (to end) _____, she (to pick) _____ him up again. After school Jack (often/not/to do) _____ his homework, he (usually/to play) _____ a game on his computer instead, or he (to lie) _____ on his bed and (to read) _____ a magazine. Then after tea, when the soaps (to start) _____, you can always find him in the living room, where he (to watch) _____ TV until he (to fall) _____ asleep.

The weekends are just the same. It's Saturday afternoon now. And what (Jack/to do) _____? (he/to play) _____ football with his friends? No, of course not.

He (to sit) _____ on the sofa in the living room and he (to watch) _____ a DVD.

Das *simple present* und das *present progressive*

Zustandsverben

Das ist wichtig!

Verben, die keine Handlung ausdrücken, sondern Meinungen, Gefühle oder Zustände, wie z. B. *to be* (sein), *to know* (kennen, wissen), *to think* (glauben, meinen), *to agree* (zustimmen), *to remember* (sich erinnern), *to understand* (verstehen), *to mean* (bedeuten), *to like* (mögen), *to love* (lieben), *to hate* (hassen), *to seem* (scheinen), *to want* (wollen), *to prefer* (bevorzugen), *to need* (brauchen), *to see* (sehen), *to hear* (hören), *to look* (aussehen), *to sound* (sich anhören, klingen), *to have* (haben im Sinne von besitzen oder Zeit/Geld haben), *to belong* (gehören)
stehen in der Regel in der **einfachen** Form.

!Merke

Zustandsverben → *simple present*.

Übung 2

Put the verb into the correct form, simple present or present progressive.

1. I (not/to know) _____ how old Jane is.
   I (to think) _____ she is 14, but I'm not sure.
2. No sorry, I can't lend you my dictionary. I (to use) _____ it myself at the moment.
3. No sorry, I can't lend you my dictionary. I (to need) _____ it myself at the moment.
4. Can I call you back in 10 minutes? We (to have) _____ lunch right now.
5. I'm sorry, I (not/to understand) _____ what you (to try) _____ to tell me.
6. What's the matter with Amy? She (not/to look) _____ very happy.
7. Ben (to think) _____ of selling his computer, but he (not/to think) _____ he will get much money for it.

Übung 3

Put the verb into the correct form, simple present or present progressive.

Robbie: Who (usually/to take) _____ the dog for a walk?

Toby: Well, my mother (always/to take) _____ him in the mornings when I (to be) _____ at school and she (sometimes/to take) _____ him in the afternoons, too, when I (not/to have) _____ time.

Robbie: And who (to take) _____ him today?

Toby: I am. (you/to want to) _____ come with me?

Robbie: I'm sorry I can't. I (to meet) _____ Jack in town at 5.30. We (to go) _____ to the cinema together.

Toby: That (to sound) _____ like a good idea. Can I come with you? The dog (only/to need) _____ a short walk today.

Robbie: OK. Let's meet at the bus stop at 5 pm. But don't be late. The bus (to leave) _____ at five past and it (usually/to run) _____ on time.

Toby: Great! See you then.

Das kann ich hier üben!	Das kann ich jetzt!	☺	😐	☹
Ich kann beide Zeitformen bilden.		☐	☐	☐
Ich weiß, wann ich welche Zeitform verwenden muss.		☐	☐	☐
Ich weiß, mit welchen Verben in der Regel nur die einfache Form, nicht aber die Verlaufsform verwendet wird.		☐	☐	☐

Zukünftiges im Englischen ausdrücken

Das kann ich hier üben!   Das kann ich jetzt!

☐ Die Bildung des *will future* und des *(be) going to future*
☐ Die richtige Verwendung beider Zeitformen
☐ Die Verwendung beider Zeitformen in Verbindung mit dem *simple present*

Bildung des *will future* und des *(be) going to future*

Das ist wichtig!

Diese Formen musst du gut beherrschen:		
	will future	**(be) going to future**
Aussage:	will do	am/are/is going to do
Verneinung:	won't do	'm not/aren't/isn't going to do
Frage:	will ... do?	am/are/is ... going to do?

Verwendung beider Zeitformen

Das ist wichtig!

Mit dem *will future* und dem *(be) going to future* berichtest du über Handlungen, die gleich oder später **passieren werden**.	
Verwende das *will future* (*I will do*)	Und das *(be) going to future* (*I'm going to do*)
wenn du **spontan entscheidest**, etwas gleich oder später zu tun.	wenn du über eine **Entscheidung** berichten willst, die **bereits feststeht**.
I'll do something = Ich habe mich während des Sprechens gerade entschieden, etwas zu tun.	*I'm going to do something* = Ich habe eine Entscheidung bereits getroffen und ich werde sie ausführen.
nach *I think, I hope, I promise, I expect, I'm sure, I'm afraid, perhaps, probably* + zukünftige Handlung.	bei einer **Vorhersage**, die mit **ziemlicher Sicherheit** eintreten wird.
bei **Tatsachen** oder **Ereignissen**, auf die du **keinen Einfluss** hast, z. B. Geburtstag.	

Verwendung beider Zeitformen

> **! Merke**
> 1. **Spontane Entscheidungen, Vermutungen** und **Tatsachen** → *will future*.
> 2. **Pläne, Absichten** oder **Vorhersagen** → *(be) going to future*.

Übung 1

Put the verb into the correct form, will future or (be) going to future.

1. It's Jack's birthday on Saturday. He (to be) __will be__ 14, so he (to invite) _____ 14 friends to a sleepover.

2. "What are your plans for this evening?" – "I (to do) _____ my homework and then I (to watch) _____ TV."

3. "I don't know if I can come to your party. I (to let) _____ you know by tomorrow."

4. I feel terrible. I think I (to be) _____ sick.

5. I feel terrible. I think I (to go and lie down) _____ for a while.

6. Tim: We need some food for the party.
   Mum: OK. I (to make) _____ some sandwiches for you.

7. Dad: Tim needs some food for the party.
   Mum: Yes, I know. I (to make) _____ some sandwiches for him.

Zukünftiges im Englischen ausdrücken

Das *will future* und das *(be) going to future* in Verbindung mit dem *simple present*

Das ist wichtig!

In Sätzen, die sich auf die Zukunft beziehen, steht das *will future* oder das *(be) going to future* **nur im Hauptsatz**. Im **Nebensatz**, der mit *when*, *if*, *before* oder *until* eingeleitet wird, steht das Verb im *simple present*.

Hauptsatz	Einleitungswort	Nebensatz
1 I'**ll invite** Tom to my party I'**m going to invite** Tom to my party	when	I **see** him.
2 I **will be** very angry with you I'**m going to be** very angry with you	if	you **lie** to me again.
3 Tom **will feed** the rabbit Tom **is going to feed** the rabbit	before	he **goes** to school.
4 We'**ll stay** here We **are going to stay** here	until	the police **arrive**.

! Merke

1. Im **Hauptsatz** steht das Verb im *will future* oder *(be) going to future*.
2. Im **Nebensatz** (nach *when/if/before/until*) steht das Verb im *simple present*.

Übung 2

Put the verb into the correct form, will future, (be) going to future or simple present.

1. When Amy (to grow up) _grows up_____, she (to be) _is going to be_____ a doctor (*feste Absicht*).

2. We (only/to go) _____ away for Christmas if we (to find) _____ a cheap hotel.

3. When Mark (to go) _____ to England next summer, he (not/to speak) _____ a word of German for two weeks. (*Das hat er bereits entschieden.*)

4. "I (not/to speak) _____ to Amy again until she (to apologize) _____ for what she said about me."

5. "Mum, I promise that I (to tidy) _____ my room before I (to go) _____ to bed."

Das will future und das (be) going to future in Verbindung mit dem simple present

6 "Jack, your room is in such a mess!" – "I know. I (to tidy) _____ it before I (to go) _____ to bed."

7 "If I (to go out) _____ before you (to get home) _____ , I (to leave) _____ a message for you on the kitchen table."

8 Kate: "Do you think you (to be allowed to) _____ stay the night at my house on Friday?"

   Jenny: "I'm not sure. I (to ask) _____ my mother when I (to get) _____ home and I (to phone) _____ you this evening."

9 Tom (to be) _____ 25 when he (to get married) _____ next year, but he (to wait) _____ until he (to be) _____ 30 before he (to have) _____ children.

Das kann ich hier üben! | **Das kann ich jetzt!**

	☺	😐	☹
Ich beherrsche die Bildung des *will future* und des *(be) going to future*.	☐	☐	☐
Ich kann diese beiden Zeitformen richtig verwenden.	☐	☐	☐
Die Verwendung der beiden Zeitformen in Verbindung mit dem *simple present* beherrsche ich.	☐	☐	☐

Das *simple past* und das *past progressive*

Das kann ich hier üben! Das kann ich jetzt!

- ☐ Die Bildung des *simple past* und des *past progressive*
- ☐ Wann man diese Zeitformen jeweils verwendet

Bildung

Das ist wichtig!

Diese Formen musst du gut beherrschen:

	simple past	past progressive
Aussage:	I did	was/were doing
Verneinung:	I didn't do	wasn't/weren't doing
Frage:	did ... do?	was/were ... doing?

Verwendung beider Zeitformen

Das ist wichtig!

Mit dem *simple past* und dem *past progressive* berichtest du über Handlungen, die in der **Vergangenheit** geschehen sind. Sie haben keinen Bezug zur Gegenwart.

Verwende das *simple past* (*I did*) für:	Und das *past progressive* (*I was doing*) für:
abgeschlossene oder **aufeinanderfolgende Handlungen** in einem vergangenen Zeitraum.	**gerade ablaufende Handlungen** in einem vergangenen Zeitraum.
Signalwörter: *yesterday*, *last year*, *ago*, *when* (+ kurze Handlung), *suddenly*, *immediately*, *at once*, *first ... then ... after that ... later* usw.	**Signalwörter:** *while*, *just* (gerade dabei), *still* (immer noch), *when* (+ lange Handlung)

Verwendung beider Zeitformen

Für Handlungen, die sich in der Vergangenheit **überschnitten** haben, verwendest du das *simple past* **in Kombination** mit dem *past progressive*:

The phone **rang** while Tom **was doing** his homework.
We **were playing** in the garden when it **started** to rain.
It **started** to rain when we **were playing** in the garden.

Die **kurze Handlung** steht im *simple past*.
Die **lange, neu eintretende Handlung** steht im *past progressive*.

> **Merke**
> 1 **Abgeschlossene/aufeinanderfolgende** Handlungen → *simple past*.
> 2 **Gerade ablaufende** Tätigkeit → *past progressive*.
> 3 **Zustandsverb** (siehe Seite 8) → *simple past*.

Übung 1

Put the verb into the correct form, simple past or past progressive.

1. While Jenny (to stay) _____ with her cousin in Vancouver last summer, they (to go on) _____ a movie tour of the city and they (to see) _____ a lot of famous actors.

2. Julian (to run) _____ up the escalator when suddenly he (to trip) _____ and (to fall) _____. Luckily, he (not/to hurt) _____ himself very badly.

3. When Amy (to go) _____ on an exchange visit to Germany last year, she (to speak) _____ German every day.

4. Harry (to cut) _____ his finger when he (to peel) _____ the potatoes.

5. The pupils (to start) _____ rehearsing for the school play at 4 pm. Five hours later they (still/to rehearse) _____.

Das *simple past* und das *past progressive*

6 When Lisa first (to meet) _____ Jenny, she (not/to like) _____ her. She (to think) _____ she was arrogant.

7 I'm sorry, I (not/to hear) _____ what you (to say) _____. I (just/to think) _____ about something else.

8 What (Tom/to wear) _____ when he (to leave) _____ the house this morning?

9 What (Tom/to wear) _____ to the party yesterday?

Übung 2

Put the verb into the correct form, simple past or past progressive.

When the teacher (to come) _____ into the classroom, everybody (to do) _____ something. Jack (to read) _____ a comic. Tim (to write) _____ a note to his girlfriend. William and Harry (to copy) _____ their homework from Ben. The twins (to chat) _____ on their mobile phones. Lucy (to sing) _____ her favourite song. Some of the pupils (to dance) _____ around the desks and others (to laugh) _____ and (to clap) _____ their hands. Nobody (to get) _____ ready for the lesson. But as soon as they (to see) _____ the teacher, everything suddenly (to go) _____ quiet. The pupils quickly (to sit down) _____ at their desks, (to open) _____ their books and (to begin) _____ to work.

Übung 3

Finish these sentences. Use the simple past or the past progressive.

1. The radio was on but nobody *(hörte zu)* _____.

2. We weren't driving very fast when the accident *(passierte)* _____.

3. It *(wurde)* _____ dark, so we turned the lights on.

4. When Tom's dad read his report, he *(wurde)* _____ angry.

5. Amy *(aß)* _____ a piece of cake when the phone rang.

6. For tea Amy *(aß)* _____ two pieces of chocolate cake.

7. When I saw Sophie last, she *(saß)* _____ in the cafeteria.

8. When I arrived at the cafeteria, Tom wasn't there. So I *(habe mich hingesetzt)* _____ and *(habe gewartet)* _____ for him.

9. *(Hast du geschlafen)* _____ when the phone rang?

10. *(Hast du geschlafen)* _____ at Tom's house last night?

	☺	😐	☹
Ich kann das *simple past* und das *past progressive* bilden.	☐	☐	☐
Ich weiß, wann ich diese Zeitformen jeweils verwende.	☐	☐	☐

Das *simple past* und das *present perfect* verglichen

Das kann ich hier üben!

- ☐ Die Bildung des *simple past* und des *present perfect*
- ☐ Wann du die jeweilige Zeitform im Englischen verwendest

Bildung

Das ist wichtig!

Diese Formen musst du gut beherrschen:		
	simple past	**present perfect simple**
Aussage:	I did	I have done/he has done
Verneinung:	I didn't do	I haven't done/he hasn't done
Frage:	did … do?	have/has … done?

Verwendung beider Zeitformen

Das ist wichtig!

Mit dem *simple past* und mit dem *present perfect* berichtest du über **Handlungen**, die **bereits geschehen** sind.	
Das *simple past* verwendest du	Das *present perfect* verwendest du
für Handlungen, die **vor langer Zeit** passiert sind.	für Handlungen, die **vor Kurzem** passiert sind.
in Verbindung **mit** einer **konkreten Zeitangabe**, z. B. „vor drei Tagen".	**ohne konkrete Zeitangabe**, z. B „eben gerade" oder „bereits".
	für Handlungen, die **von der Vergangenheit bis jetzt** andauern, z. B. „jemals", „noch nie", „immer schon" usw.
	für Handlungen, die **heute** oder **diese Woche geschehen** sind bzw. **noch nicht geschehen** sind.

Verwendung beider Zeitformen

Signalwörter:
yesterday, (2 days) ago, when, what time, in (2003), last week, last year etc.

Signalwörter:
just, already, ever, never (noch nie), always (immer schon), yet, not yet, before, today, this week, so far (bis jetzt), since, for (seit) etc.

! Merke

1 **Abgeschlossene** Handlung in einem **vergangenen Zeitraum** → simple past.
2 **Abgeschlossene** Handlung mit **Bezug zur Gegenwart** → present perfect.

Übung 1

Put the verb into the correct form, simple past or present perfect.

1. Ben can't go swimming. He (to break) _____ his arm.

2. Ben can't go swimming. He (to break) _____ his arm yesterday.

3. Tom (finish) _____ his German homework before tea, but he (not/to finish) _____ his Maths homework yet.

4. Kate (to be born) _____ in South Africa but her parents (to move) _____ to Britain when she (to be) _____ one year old. So she (to spend) _____ most of her life there.

5. Mrs Wallace is the best English teacher we (ever/to have) _____. The teacher we (to have) _____ last year (not/to be) _____ very good. We (not/to learn) _____ much with her.

6. (you/to be) _____ to the new Italian restaurant that (just/to open) _____ in Main St? – Yes, I have. I (have) _____ lunch there last week. It (to be) _____ very good.

Das *simple past* und das *present perfect* verglichen

Übung 2

Put the verb into the correct form, simple past or present perfect.

1. Mr Winter (to start) _____ work at 8 o'clock this morning.

2. Mr Winter (to be) _____ at the office since 8 o'clock this morning.

3. How's Lucy? – I really don't know. I (not/to see) _____ her for a long time. But the last time I (to speak) _____ to her she was fine.

4. Tom (to meet) _____ his girlfriend soon after he (to move) _____ to San Diego.

5. Tom (to know) _____ his girlfriend since he (to move) _____ to San Diego.

6. Ben last (to see) _____ his grandparents at Christmas.

7. Ben (not/to see) _____ his grandparents since Christmas.

8. Where's Mum? – She (to go) _____ shopping. She (to leave) _____ the house about five minutes ago.

9. The phone bill (to go down) _____ since Daniel (to break up) _____ with his girlfriend.

10. The phone bill (to go down) _____ since Daniel (to have to) _____ pay for all his own calls.

Verwendung beider Zeitformen

Übung 3

Make questions. Use the simple past or the present perfect.

1. Is it the band's first concert in Germany or (they/to play) _____ here before?

2. Lily is in the living room. – Oh! When (she/to arrive) _____? Why (you/not/to tell) _____ me that she was here?

3. How long (it/to take) _____ you to do your homework yesterday?

4. How long (you/to be) _____ at your school?

5. Amy: I like your new jacket. Where (you/to buy) _____ it?

   Ellie: At the new boutique in the shopping mall. (you/ever/to be) _____ there?

6. Please don't pull the dog's tail. How many times (I/to tell) _____ you that he doesn't like it.

Das kann ich hier üben! | **Das kann ich jetzt!**

	☺	😐	☹
Ich beherrsche die Bildung des *simple past* und des *present perfect*.	☐	☐	☐
Ich weiß, wann ich die jeweilige Zeitform im Englischen verwende.	☐	☐	☐

Das *present perfect progressive*

> **Das kann ich hier üben!** | **Das kann ich jetzt!**
> - ❏ Die Bildung des *present perfect progressive*
> - ❏ Die Verwendung dieser Zeitform im Englischen

Bildung

Das ist wichtig!

Diese Formen musst du gut beherrschen:	
	present perfect progressive
Aussage:	*I have been doing/he has been doing*
Verneinung:	*I haven't been doing/he hasn't been doing*
Frage:	*have … been doing?/has … been doing?*

Verwendung

Das ist wichtig!

Das *present perfect progressive (I have been doing)* verwendest du für **Tätigkeiten**, die **in der Vergangenheit begonnen** haben und **bis jetzt** (und möglicherweise auch **in der Zukunft**) noch **andauern**:

1. Wie lange (seit wann) wartest du (schon)?
   How long have you **been waiting**?

2. Ich warte seit einer halben Stunde/seit 2 Uhr/den ganzen Vormittag.
   I **have been waiting for** half an hour now/**since** 2 o'clock/**all** morning.

> **❗ Merke**
>
> 1. Mit dem *present perfect progressive* sagst du, **wie lange** eine **Tätigkeit bereits** am Laufen ist.
> 2. Häufige **Signalwörter** hierfür sind:
>   *since* + Zeitpunkt (z. B. *since yesterday/last week/2005/breakfast* usw.)
>   *for* + Zeitraum (z. B. *for 10 minutes/hours/days/weeks/years* usw.)
>   *all morning/afternoon/evening/day* usw.

Verwendung

Übung 1

Put in since or for.

1. **since** 2 o'clock
2. **for** five hours
3. _____ yesterday
4. _____ last summer
5. _____ two minutes
6. _____ years
7. _____ Christmas
8. _____ a long time
9. _____ the beginning of the year
10. _____ ages
11. _____ he was little
12. _____ as long as I can remember

Übung 2

Put in since or for.

1. Ben has been playing on the Wii …
   a) _for_ 2 hours.
   b) _since_ 3 o'clock.

2. Jenny has been learning German …
   a) _____ two years.
   b) _____ Year 7.

3. The girls have been rehearsing for their school play …
   a) _____ the beginning of the year.
   b) _____ two months.

4. Jack has got a new girlfriend. He has been going out with her …
   a) _____ last Wednesday.
   b) _____ almost a week.

5. Katie has been singing with the band …
   a) _____ as long as I can remember.
   b) _____ 2005.

6. They have been touring the country …
   a) _____ August.
   b) _____ three months.

Das *present perfect progressive*

Übung 3

Put in the correct form of the verb and since or for or all.

1. We (to learn) _have been learning_ English _since_ primary school.

2. Julia (to research) _____ her project on the Internet _____ afternoon.

3. Harry and Tom (to sit) _____ in front of the TV _____ they got home from school.

4. My uncle and aunt (to go) _____ to Thailand for their holidays _____ as long as I can remember.

5. The two girls (to have) _____ riding lessons _____ they were little.

6. Sophie (to sing) _____ in the school choir _____ she was ten years old.

7. Grandma (to live) _____ next door to us _____ Grandpa died.

8. The two girls (to gossip) _____ on the phone _____ morning.

9. Tom (to go out) _____ with his girlfriend _____ they met on holiday last year.

10. Kate (to text) _____ me every single day _____ the last six months.

Verwendung

Übung 4

Put in the correct form of the verb, present progressive or present perfect progressive.

1. Tom (to read) _is reading_ a book at the moment. It must be good because he (to read) _has been reading_ it all afternoon.

2. I (to wait) _____ for a Number 9 bus into town. I (to wait) _____ for almost half an hour now.

3. The neighbours (to have) _____ another party on Saturday. They (to have) _____ parties all summer.

4. "Please don't disturb Tom." – "Why? What (he/to do) _____?" – "He (to try) _____ to do his homework but he (not/to get) _____ on very well with it."

5. "I haven't seen you for a long time. What (you/to do) _____?" – "Oh, you know me. I (to keep) _____ myself busy."

Das kann ich hier üben!	Das kann ich jetzt!	😊	😐	☹
Ich beherrsche die Bildung des *present perfect progressive*.		☐	☐	☐
Ich weiß, wie diese Zeitform im Englischen verwendet wird.		☐	☐	☐

Das *present perfect simple* und das *present perfect progressive* verglichen

Das kann ich hier üben!

- ☐ Die Bildung beider Zeitformen
- ☐ Die Verwendung dieser Zeitformen

Bildung

Das ist wichtig!

Diese Formen musst du gut beherrschen:		
	present perfect simple	**present perfect progressive**
Aussage:	*I have done/* *he has done*	*I have been doing/* *he has been doing*
Verneinung:	*I haven't done/* *he hasn't done*	*I haven't done/* *he hasn't been doing*
Frage:	*have/has ... done?*	*have/has ... been doing?*

Verwendung beider Zeitformen

Das ist wichtig!

Mit dem *present perfect simple* und dem *present perfect progressive* berichtest du über Handlungen, die einen Bezug sowohl zur Vergangenheit als auch zur Gegenwart haben.

Das *present perfect simple* verwendest du für:	Das *present perfect progressive* verwendest du für:
abgeschlossene Handlungen.	Tätigkeiten, die **bis jetzt** noch **andauern**.
Handlungen in Verbindung mit **ever, never, always**.	Tätigkeiten in Verbindung mit **since, for** (seit) oder **all morning/day/week** usw.
Handlungen in Verbindung mit einer **Zahl**.	
Signalwörter: always, never, ever, yet, already, just once/twice/three times ...	**Signalwörter:** since/for all day/week/year

Verwendung beider Zeitformen

Vergleiche:
1 Tom **has tidied** his room.
 Tom **has been tidying** his room **since** 9 am.
2 The phone **has rung 10 times** today.
 The phone **has been ringing all** day.

> **Merke**
> 1 **Abgeschlossene** Handlungen → *present perfect simple*.
> 2 Handlungen in Verbindung mit **ever/never/always** → *present perfect simple*.
> 3 Handlungen in Verbindung mit einer **Zahl** → *present perfect simple*.
> 4 Tätigkeiten **bis jetzt** → *present perfect progressive*.
> 5 Tätigkeiten in Verbindung mit **since/for** oder **all morning/day/week** → *present perfect progressive*.

Übung 1

Put in the correct form of the verb, present perfect simple or present perfect progressive.

1 You (to watch) _____ TV for three hours now. Please turn the TV off now.

2 Jack is always late. I don't think he (ever/to arrive) _____ anywhere on time.

3 The weather is terrible. It (to rain) _____ all week.

4 The film was very funny. I (never/to laugh) _____ so much in my life.

5 Kate (to make) _____ her bed and she (to put) _____ her dirty clothes in the washing, but she (not/to tidy) _____ her desk yet.

6 You (to play) _____ on the Wii all evening. Can't you do something else now?

7 We're having a garden party on Saturday. We (to invite) _____ 50 people.

Das *present perfect simple* und das *present perfect progressive* verglichen

8 I think Kate should go and see a doctor. She (to cough = husten)
   _____ all week.

9 Oh Lucy, there you are at last. I (to try) _____ to phone you all day.

10 Oh Lucy, there you are at last. I (to try) _____ to phone you at least ten times today.

Übung 2

Put in the correct form of the verb, present perfect simple or present perfect progressive, and since or for where necessary.

> **TIPP**
> Zustandsverben (siehe Seite 8) stehen in der einfachen Form.

1 Ben (to want) _____ to become an actor _____ he was in his first school play.

2 Lucy and Olivia (to e-mail) _____ each other _____ they met on holiday last year.

3 Our English teacher is ill at the moment. She (not/to be) _____ at school _____ last week.

4 The band (to have) _____ a lot of success _____ their first hit in 2005.

5 They (to raise) _____ money for charity _____ as long as I can remember.

6 How long (the children/to practise) _____ _____ for the school concert?

7 How long (Amy/to be) _____ a fan of hip hop music?

Verwendung beider Zeitformen

8 Mum: Ben, you (to be) _____ at home for three hours now. What (you/to do) _____ all this time?

Ben: I (to text) _____ my friends, I (to surf) _____ the Internet, I (to play) _____ on the Wii. And yes, Mum, you are right again. I (not/to start) _____ to do my homework yet.

9 The teacher (to talk about) _____ the present perfect for two weeks now, but not all the pupils (to understand) _____ it yet. And what about you? (you/to understand) _____ it yet?

Das kann ich hier üben!	Das kann ich jetzt!			
		🙂	😐	☹
Ich beherrsche die Bildung der beiden Zeitformen.		☐	☐	☐
Ich weiß, wie die beiden Zeitformen im Englischen verwendet werden.		☐	☐	☐

Das *past perfect simple* und das *past perfect progressive* verglichen

Das kann ich hier üben!   Das kann ich jetzt!

- ❏ Die Bildung beider Zeitformen
- ❏ Die Verwendung dieser Zeitformen

Bildung
Das ist wichtig!

Diese Formen musst du gut beherrschen:		
	simple past	past perfect simple/progressive
Aussage:	did	had done/had been doing
Verneinung:	didn't do	hadn't done/hadn't been doing
Frage:	did ... do?	had ... done/had ... been doing?

Verwendung beider Zeitformen
Das ist wichtig!

Das *past perfect* (*simple* und *progressive*) wird meist **in Verbindung** mit dem *simple past* verwendet.

simple past	past perfect
	past perfect simple: waren die Einbrecher bereits verschwunden. the burglars **had** already **disappeared**.
Bis die Polizei ankam, By the time the police **arrived**,	
	past perfect progressive: hatte ich bereits 2 Stunden lang gewartet. I **had been waiting** for two hours.

Verwendung beider Zeitformen

> **Merke**
> 1 **Einfache** Vergangenheit → *simple past*.
> 2 **Kurze** Handlungen in der Vorvergangenheit → *past perfect simple*.
> 3 **Lange** Handlungen in der Vorvergangenheit → *past perfect progressive*.
> 4 Das Plusquamperfekt bildest du mit „hatten" oder „waren" + Partizip. Das *past perfect* bildest du **nur** mit *had* + Partizip (**niemals** mit *was/were!*).

Übung 1

Put in the correct form of the verb, simple past or past perfect simple.

1. When Kate got home, she (to be) __was__ hungry.

2. When Kate got home, she (to be) __was__ hungry because she (not/to eat) __hadn't eaten__ anything all day.

3. Tim couldn't go swimming last Saturday because he (to have) _____ a cold.

4. Tim couldn't play football last Saturday because he (to break) _____ a bone in his foot.

5. I couldn't open the door because I (not/to have) _____ a key.

6. I couldn't open the door because I (to lose) _____ my key.

7. Jack was surprised when Tom (to invite) _____ him to his party because he (not/to hear) _____ from him for a long time.

8. Jack was surprised when Tom (to invite) _____ him to his party because he (to think) _____ he (not/to like) _____ him.

Das *past perfect simple* und das *past perfect progressive* verglichen

Übung 2

Put in the correct form of the verb, past perfect simple or past perfect progressive.

1. Ben didn't want to go to the cinema again. He (already/to see) _____ the film twice.

2. The boys (only/to play) _____ football in the park for about ten minutes when it started to rain.

3. Katie wasn't sure if she wanted to audition for a role in the school play. She (not/to make up) _____ her mind.

4. After she (to have) _____ toothache for about a week, Kate went to see the dentist.

5. The singer was exhausted¹ because she (to tour) _____ the country for two months.

6. The singer was exhausted because she (to give) _____ ten concerts in the last two months.

Übung 3

Put in the correct form of the verb, past perfect simple or past perfect progressive.

When Katie arrived at the cafeteria, Daniel (already/to wait) _____ for twenty minutes. After they (to have) _____ something to eat and drink, they decided to go to the park to play mini-golf.

They (to play) _____ mini-golf for about half an hour when Katie asked Daniel if he (to notice) _____ that a man (to watch) _____ them ever since they

---
1 *exhausted* = erschöpft

Verwendung beider Zeitformen

(to arrive) _____ there. When Daniel said that he (to

see) _____ him at the cafeteria and was sure that he

(to follow) _____ them to the park, Katie was

worried. After they (to finish) _____ the game,
which Katie won easily, they walked quickly back to town. They (only/to look)

_____ at the computer games in a
large department store for about five minutes when suddenly they saw

him again. He (to follow) _____ them back
to town. Daniel and Katie had no idea who he was. They (never/to see)

_____ him before.

Das kann ich hier üben!	Das kann ich jetzt!	☺	😐	☹
Ich beherrsche die Bildung des *past perfect simple* und des *past perfect progressive*.		☐	☐	☐
Ich weiß, wie diese Zeitformen im Englischen verwendet werden.		☐	☐	☐

Modale Hilfsverben mit dem Infinitiv Präsens und dem Infinitiv Perfekt

Das kann ich hier üben! Das kann ich jetzt!

- ❏ Die Bildung des Infinitiv Perfekt
- ❏ Die Verwendung der modalen Hilfsverben mit dem Infinitiv Präsens und dem Infinitiv Perfekt

Bildung

Das ist wichtig!

Modale Hilfsverben sind Wörter wie *can, may, must, needn't, could, might, should* und *ought to*. Sie können mit einem **Infinitiv Präsens** (**ohne** *to*) oder mit einem **Infinitiv Perfekt** verwendet werden. Schau dir diese Beispiele an:

Modales Hilfsverb + Infinitiv Präsens	Modales Hilfsverb + Infinitiv Perfekt
Ben **muss** nach Hause **gehen**. Ben **must go** home.	Ben **muss** nach Hause **gegangen sein**. Ben **must have gone** home.
Amy **muss** Jack nicht **anrufen**. Amy **needn't phone** Jack.	Amy **hätte** Jack **nicht anrufen müssen**. Amy **needn't have phoned** Jack.
Du **könntest** Tom **fragen**. You **could ask** Jack.	Du **hättest** Tom **fragen können**. You **could have asked** Jack.
Er **könnte** dir vielleicht **helfen**. He **might be able** to help you.	Er **hätte** dir vielleicht **helfen können**. He **might have been able** to help you.

!**Merke**

Der Infinitiv Perfekt wird mit *have* + Verb in der 3. Form gebildet (**niemals** mit *be*).

Übung 1

Rewrite these sentences using the perfect infinitive.

1. You should call the police.

    <u>You should have called the police.</u>

Bildung

2 We might be late.
_____

3 They must know the truth.
_____

4 We ought to leave before lunch.
_____

5 Tom can't say that.
_____

6 Jack could fly to New York.
_____

7 You needn't do that.
_____

Übung 2

Complete these sentences using the present infinitive or the perfect infinitive.

1 Why don't you ask Tom. He may (to help) _help_ you.

2 Why didn't you ask Tom. He might (to help) _have helped_ you.

3 The lights were on and I could hear voices, so they must (to be) _____ at home.

4 You shouldn't (to tell) _____ Kate what I said. She will be angry with me now.

5 We ought to (to leave) _____ now. It's getting late.

6 If they had told you the truth, what would you (to do) _____?

7 We had no idea that the river was inhabited by crocodiles. The locals could (to warn) _____ us not to swim there.

Modale Hilfsverben mit dem Infinitiv Präsens und dem Infinitiv Perfekt

Übung 3

Rewrite these questions using the perfect infinitive.

1. What could I say?

   What could I have said?

2. How should Amy react?

   How

3. Who could I ask?

4. Why must Tom know?

5. Where can I put my shoes?

Übung 4

Translate the words in brackets.

1. Bringing up three children on her own *(muss schwierig gewesen sein.)*

2. Ben isn't home yet. *(Vielleicht hat er den Bus verpasst.)*

3. We've got plenty of time, so you *(musst dich nicht beeilen.)*

4. Amy looks very happy. She *(muss eine gute Note in der Arbeit bekommen haben.)*

Übung 5

Translation practice.

1. Tom muss mich gesehen haben.

2. Ben kann nicht nach Hause gegangen sein.

3. Ich hätte einen Arzt rufen sollen.

4. Du hättest mich fragen können.

5. Sie hätten vielleicht Angst gehabt.

6. Was hätte ich sagen können?

7. Du hättest mir eine SMS schicken können.

8. Du hättest nicht warten müssen.

9. Wir hätten etwas im Restaurant essen können.

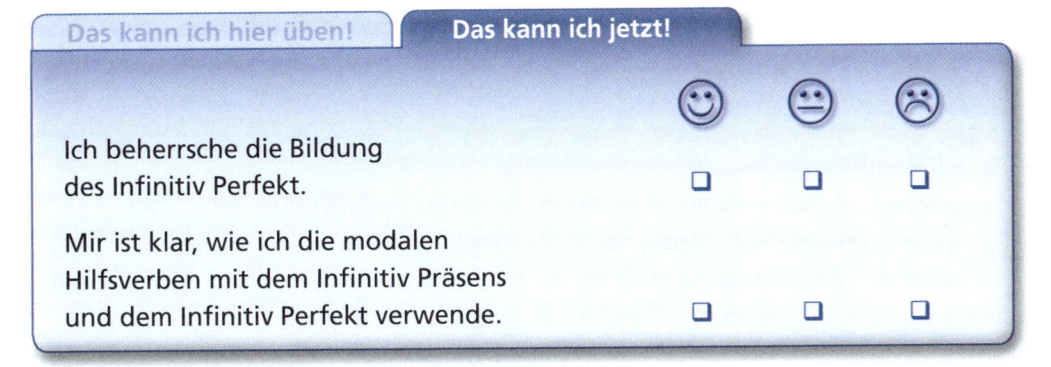

Das kann ich hier üben! | **Das kann ich jetzt!**

	☺	😐	☹
Ich beherrsche die Bildung des Infinitiv Perfekt.	☐	☐	☐
Mir ist klar, wie ich die modalen Hilfsverben mit dem Infinitiv Präsens und dem Infinitiv Perfekt verwende.	☐	☐	☐

Bedingungssätze vom Typ I, II und III

Das kann ich hier üben!   Das kann ich jetzt!

- Wie ein Bedingungssatz aufgebaut ist
- Welche Typen von Bedingungssätzen es gibt
- Wie man Bedingungssätze vom Typ I, II und III bildet und verwendet
- Wie man Bedingungssätze vom Typ I mit modalem Hilfsverb oder mit Imperativ bildet
- Wie man einen Bedingungssatz vom Typ III mit einem Bedingungssatz vom Typ II kombinieren kann

Was muss ich über Bedingungssätze wissen?
Das ist wichtig!

1. Ein Bedingungssatz besteht aus **zwei** Teilen: einem **Hauptsatz** und einem **Nebensatz mit *if*.**
2. Der *if*-Satz kann **vor oder nach** dem Hauptsatz stehen.
3. Wenn der Bedingungssatz **mit dem *if*-Satz anfängt**, musst du ein **Komma** zwischen die beiden Sätze setzen.
4. Es gibt **drei Grundtypen** von Bedingungssätzen.

Bildung der Bedingungssätze vom Typ I, II und III
Das ist wichtig!

Schau dir diese Beispiele an:

Typ I:	If Tom **finds** a job, he **will earn** some money.
Typ II:	If Tom **found** a job, he **would earn** some money.
Typ III:	If Tom **had found** a job, he **would have earned** some money.

> **!Merke**
>
> Bedingungssatz vom
> Typ I: *if*-Satz → **simple present**, Hauptsatz → **will future**.
> Typ II: *if*-Satz → **simple past**   , Hauptsatz → **would + infinitive**.
> Typ III: *if*-Satz → **past perfect** , Hauptsatz → **would have + 3. Verbform**.

Bildung der Bedingungssätze vom Typ I, II und III

Übung 1

Put the verbs into the correct form, simple present or will future.

> **TIPP**
> Das Verb im *if*-Satz steht im *simple present*, also **vergiss nicht** das *-(e)s* bei der 3. Person Singular (*he, she, it*).

1 If Tom (to go) _____ to bed late, he (to feel) _____ tired tomorrow.

2 If he (to be) _____ tired tomorrow, he (not/to be able to) _____ concentrate in class.

3 If he (not/to concentrate) _____ in class, he (not/to understand) _____ what the teacher is talking about and he (not/to be able to) _____ do his homework.

4 If he (not/to do) _____ his homework again, he (to get) _____ into trouble and his teacher (to give) _____ him another bad mark.

5 If he (to get) _____ another bad mark, his parents (not/to be) _____ happy and he (to be grounded[1]) _____.

6 If Tom (to be grounded) _____, he (not/to be) _____ happy either because he (not/to be able to) _____ meet his new girlfriend.

So the best thing for Tom to do is to go to bed early, don't you think?

---
1 *to be grounded* = Hausarrest bekommen

Bedingungssätze vom Typ I, II und III

Übung 2

Put the verbs into the correct form, simple past or conditional II (would + infinitive).

1. If Katie (to have) _____ a dog, she (to take) _____ him for a walk every day.

2. If she (to take) _____ him for a walk every day, she (not/to waste) _____ so much time watching TV.

3. If she (not/to waste) _____ so much time watching TV, she (probably/to do) _____ better at school.

4. If she (to do) _____ better at school, she (to enjoy) _____ it more and she (to have) _____ more self-confidence.

5. If she (to have) _____ more self-confidence, the other children (not/to bully) _____ her and she (to be) _____ more popular.

6. If she (to be) _____ more popular, she (to be) _____ much happier and she (to enjoy) _____ life more.

7. If she (to enjoy) _____ life more, she (not/to be) _____ so bad-tempered.

8. So if I (to be) _____ Katie's parents, I (to get) _____ her a dog.

Übung 3

Put the verbs into the correct form, past perfect or conditional III (would have + 3. Verbform).

1. If my mother (not/to meet) _____ your mother yesterday, she (never/to find out) _____ about the party.

2. If she (not/to find out) _____ about the party, I (not/to be grounded) _____.

3. If I (not/to be grounded) _____, I (to be allowed to) _____ go to the disco.

4. If I (to be allowed to) _____ go to the disco, I (to go) _____ with Amy.

5. I'm sure Amy (to say) _____ "Yes" if I (to ask) _____ her to go with me.

6. So, you see, if you (not/to tell) _____ your mother about the party and she (not/to meet) _____ my mother yesterday, I (to be able to) _____ go to the disco with Amy and I (to be) _____ the happiest person alive and this disaster in my life (never/to happen) _____.

Bedingungssätze vom Typ I, II und III

Übung 4

Finish these sentences with the verb in the correct form. Use type I, II or III.

1 I'll lend you my new DVD if you (to promise) _____ to give it back to me tomorrow.

2 If we had a garden, we (to grow) _____ our own vegetables.

3 I (to send) _____ you a text message if I miss the train.

4 The dog wouldn't be so fat if he (to get) _____ more exercise.

5 Dad wouldn't have got a parking ticket if he (not/to park) _____ the car in a no-parking zone.

6 If we didn't have a car, we (to have to) _____ go by train.

7 If my mother had studied French instead of German at university, she (never/to meet) _____ my father.

8 I wouldn't have been late for school this morning if I (not/to forget) _____ to set my alarm clock.

9 The holiday won't be too expensive if we (to stay) _____ at youth hostels.

10 If I had known that it was a secret, I (not/to tell) _____ anybody.

11 If we book the holiday on the Internet, (it/to make) _____ a difference in price?

Übung 5

Finish these sentences with the more suitable form of "if-clause", type I, II or III.

1. The Browns aren't poor. If they (to be) _____ poor, they (not/to be able to) _____ send their children to private schools.

2. My parents are thinking of emigrating to Australia, but we (only/to move) _____ there if my father (to find) _____ a good job.

3. Why didn't you ask Dad if you could borrow his camera? If you (to ask) _____ him, I'm sure he (to lend) _____ it to you.

4. That potato salad has been in the sun too long. I (not/to eat) _____ if I (to be) _____ you.

5. I'm glad that we live in a town. If we (to live) _____ in the country, we (to have to) _____ travel miles to reach the nearest shops.

6. The village was difficult to find. If we (not/to have) _____ a satnav, he (never/to find) _____ it.

Bedingungssätze vom Typ I, II und III

Bedingungssatz Typ I mit modalem Hilfsverb oder mit Imperativ

Das ist wichtig!

Schau dir diese Beispiele an:

Typ I: If you get home late tonight, you **can have** a lie in tomorrow morning.
I **may be**[2] asleep./I **might**[2] be asleep.
you **should go** to bed early tomorrow.
please **don't make** too much noise.

! Merke

Beim Bedingungssatz vom Typ I kann im **Hauptsatz** auch ein **modales Hilfsverb** oder der **Imperativ** stehen.

Übung 6

Put the verbs into the correct form. Use the simple present in the if-clause, and

~~can~~, can't, must, mustn't, needn't, may/might, should + infinitive
or an imperative

in the main clause.

1 If you (not/to like) _don't like_____ the shoes here, we (to go) _can go_____ to another shop.

2 If you (not/to keep) _____ your dog on a lead, he (to chase) _____ the sheep in the fields.

3 If you (to be) _____ hungry, please (to help) _____ yourselves to the biscuits.

4 You (to post) _____ the birthday card today if you (to want) _____ it to arrive on time.

5 You (to be) _____ rude to people if you (to want) _____ them to help you.

6 That restaurant (to be) _____ any good if nobody ever (to eat) _____ there.

---
2 *may* oder *might* steht oft für „vielleicht" oder „möglicherweise".

7 You (to meet) _____ us at the airport if you (not/to have) _____ time. We can take the train.

8 If you (to need) _____ any help, (not/to be afraid) _____ to ask me.

9 If you (to chat) _____ to somebody online who you don't know, you (never/to tell) _____ him/her your real name.

Bedingungssatz Typ III in Kombination mit Bedingungssatz Typ II

Das ist wichtig!

Der Bedingungssatz **Typ III** kann (wie im Deutschen) auch **in Kombination** mit dem Bedingungssatz **Typ II** gebildet werden:

Wenn Leona Lewis die Castingshow nicht **gewonnen hätte**,
wäre sie wahrscheinlich heute kein internationaler Star.
If Leona Lewis **hadn't won** the casting show,
she probably **wouldn't be** an international star today.

!Merke

Bei Typ III ist manchmal im **Hauptsatz** auch *would + infinitive* möglich.

Übung 7

Put the verbs in the correct form. Decide whether you need conditional I or conditional II.

1 If you had gone to bed earlier last night, you (not/to be) _____ tired today.

2 If Mum hadn't forgotten to close all the windows, we (not/to have to) _____ turn back.

3 If you had had a drink at the restaurant, you (not/to be) _____ thirsty now.

4 If we had been able to get a flight, we (to spend) _____ the weekend in New York.

Bedingungssätze vom Typ I, II und III

5   If Amy had learnt to dance when she was young, she (can/to be)

    _____ a star today.

6   If Ruby hadn't read the problem page in her favourite teen magazine, she

    (not/to know) _____ how to react to the bullies
    at her school.

7   If you had done your homework earlier, you (to be able to)

    _____ watch TV now.

8   If the police had arrived sooner, they (might/to catch)

    _____ the burglars.

Übung 8

Translation practice: Conditional sentences Type I, II and III.

1   Sie würden sehr enttäuscht sein, wenn sie den Wettbewerb nicht
    gewinnen würden.

    _____

    _____

2   Wenn du mich gefragt hättest, hätte ich dir geholfen.

    _____

    _____

3   Wenn du gefrühstückt hättest, würdest du jetzt nicht hungrig sein.

    _____

    _____

4   Wenn der Mann etwas langsamer gesprochen hätte, hätte ich ihn vielleicht
    verstanden.

    _____

    _____

Bedingungssatz Typ III in Kombination mit Bedingungssatz Typ II

5   Wenn du Tom jetzt sehen würdest, würdest du einen Schock bekommen.

_____

_____

6   Wenn es mir morgen nicht besser geht, gehe ich zum Arzt.

_____

_____

7   Was hättest du gemacht, wenn der Bus nicht gekommen wäre?

_____

_____

Das kann ich hier üben!	**Das kann ich jetzt!**	☺	😐	☹
Ich weiß, wie ein Bedingungssatz aufgebaut ist.		❑	❑	❑
Mir ist klar, welche Typen von Bedingungssätzen es gibt.		❑	❑	❑
Ich weiß, wie ich Bedingungssätze vom Typ I, II und III bilde und verwende.		❑	❑	❑
Mir ist klar, wie man Bedingungssätze vom Typ I mit modalem Hilfsverb oder mit Imperativ bildet.		❑	❑	❑
Ich weiß, wie man einen Bedingungssatz vom Typ III mit einem Bedingungssatz vom Typ II kombinieren kann.		❑	❑	❑

Alle Zeitformen auf einen Blick

Das kann ich hier üben!   **Das kann ich jetzt!**

- ❑ Die Verwendung der *present and future tenses*
- ❑ Die Verwendung der *past and past perfect tenses*

Present, present perfect and future tenses

Das ist wichtig!

present	I do	I am doing
present perfect	I have done	I have been doing
future	I will do	I'm going to do

Übung 1

Put the verb into the correct form.

Mum: What are your plans for this evening?

Ellie: I (to go) _____ to the cinema with Harry. We (to meet) _____ outside the Odeon at 7.30. The film (to start) _____ at 8.

Mum: And what time (it/to finish) _____ ?

Ellie: No idea, but I'm sure it (not/to be) _____ late.

Übung 2

Put the verb into the correct form.

Ben: What (you/to do) _____, Harry?

Harry: I (to watch) _____ those workmen over there. In fact, I (to watch) _____ them for over three hours now and they (even/not/to start) _____ to work yet!

Present, present perfect and future tenses

Übung 3

Put the verb into the correct form.

Jack (to learn) _____ to drive now. He (to have) _____ driving lessons since Christmas. He (to have) _____ 20 lessons so far. He (to take) _____ his driving test on Thursday.

Übung 4

Put the verb into the correct form.

Lily: What (you/to do) _____ this evening?

Emily: I (to go) _____ to Paris for the weekend. My parents (to take) _____ me to Disneyland.

Lily: Lucky you! How (you/to get) _____ there?

Emily: We (to fly) _____. Our flight (to leave) _____ at 9 pm.

Lily: I (to ask) _____ my mum if she can take you to the airport if you (to like) _____.

Emily: No, it's OK, thanks. My brother (to drive) _____ us.

Alle Zeitformen auf einen Blick

Past, present perfect and past perfect tenses

Das ist wichtig!

past	I did	I was doing
present perfect	I have done	I have been doing
past perfect	I had done	I had been doing

Übung 5

Put the verb into the correct form.

1 When Ellie arrived at the cinema, Jack (to wait for)

   _____ her.

2 When Ellie arrived at the cinema, Jack (to wait for)

   _____ her for twenty minutes.

3 I went into the shop because I (to look for) _____
   a birthday present for my best friend.

4 I went into the shop because I (to know) _____
   the shop assistants there.

5 I went into the shop because I (to see) _____
   their advertisement in the newspaper.

6 I woke up at 6 o'clock this morning because my dog (to bark)

   _____ loudly.

7 I woke up at 6 o'clock this morning, looked at the clock and then (to go

   back) _____ to sleep again.

8 I woke up at 6 o'clock this morning because I (to be)

   _____ cold. I (to forget)

   _____ to shut the window.

9 The fans reacted very badly when they (to hear)

   _____ that the band (to want)

   _____ to split up.

Past, present perfect and past perfect tenses

10 The fans reacted very badly when they (to hear) _____ that the band (to decide) _____ to split up.

Übung 6

Put the verb into the correct form.

The Titanic (to lie) _____ on the bottom of the ocean since 1912. It (to sink) _____ on its maiden voyage from Southampton to New York. When the ship (to hit) _____ the ice-berg, the passengers and the crew (not/to panic) _____ at first. By the time they (to realize) _____ that the ship (to sink) _____, it was too late. Most of the lifeboats (already/to leave) _____ half-full. 1,503 people (to lose) _____ their lives in the tragedy.

Übung 7

Put the verb into the correct form.

When I (to get) _____ home from work on Monday, I (to open) _____ the front door and (to step) _____ into a pool of water which (to come) _____ out from under the kitchen door. The hose on my dish-washer (to burst) _____. The engineer (to promise) _____ to come and mend it straightaway, but that (to be) _____ four days ago and I (not/to hear) _____ from him since.

Alle Zeitformen auf einen Blick

Übung 8

Put the verb into the correct form.

I (to dive) _____ off the coast of Florida when I (to come across) _____ George, the resident shark. The diving instructor (to warn) _____ me about him, so, of course, I (to know) _____ immediately that he (to be) _____ harmless. But in that terrifying moment as he (to swim) _____ directly towards me, I suddenly (to begin) _____ to wonder whether he (to know) _____ that, too.

Übung 9

Put the verb into the correct form.

J. K. Rowling (to begin) _____ her writing life as a single mother who (to live) _____ on state benefits[1]. But soon the magical characters that she (to create) _____ in her Harry Potter books (to shoot) _____ her to international stardom and by 2001 she (to become) _____ the highest-paid woman in Britain. Yet despite her enormous success, J. K. Rowling (to keep) _____ her feet firmly on the ground. Today, she (to live) _____ in Scotland with her second husband, who (to be) _____ a doctor.

---

1   state benefits = Sozialhilfe

Übung 10

Put the verb into the correct tense.

Amy: Lucy, there you are at last! Where (you/to be) _____? I (to wait) _____ for you for fifteen minutes. We (to arrange) _____ to meet here at 3 o'clock, remember?

Lucy: Oh I'm sorry. I (just/to pass) _____ that new boutique that (just/to open) _____ on the corner when I (to see) _____ a really nice T-shirt in the window. I (to look for) _____ one like that for weeks, so I (to think) _____ I must just go in and try it on. Look, here it is. What (you/to think) _____ of it?

Amy: It (to look) _____ great. You (not/to believe) _____ it but I (to buy) _____ exactly the same T-shirt from that same shop yesterday.

Übung 11

Put the verb into the correct tense.

Every month I (to send) _____ an e-mail to my e-friend in England. Last week I (to tell) _____ her about our class trip to Freiburg. We all (to enjoy) _____ it so much and it (to be) _____ great to have a whole week without any lessons!

At the moment I (to revise) _____ for our next English test. We (to have) _____ it on Friday. I (not/

Alle Zeitformen auf einen Blick

to learn) _____ so much for a long time and I hope it (not/to be) _____ too difficult.

I (to sit) _____ at my desk since 5 o'clock. I couldn't start working before because I (to forget) _____ to take my front door key with me, so I (to have to) _____ wait for my parents to come home from work first. But as soon as I (to finish) _____ tea, I (to go) _____ up to my room.

It (to be) _____ 8 o'clock now, so that means I (to work) _____ for three hours. I (to think) _____ I (to go) _____ to bed. I (to do) _____ enough for today.

Übung 12

Put the verb into the correct tense.

Two owls or two twits? (*Zwei Eulen oder zwei Trottel?*)

Mr Brown has been keen on owls since childhood, so he (to be) _____ very excited one day last week when he (to hear) _____ that some owls (to build) _____ their nest in the woods nearby.

That night he (to decide) _____ to try his luck. At 11 pm he (to go) _____ out into his garden and (to begin) _____ to hoot. "Twit...to...woo," he (to call)

Past, present perfect and past perfect tenses

_____. "Twit...to...woo," came the immediate reply.

Mr Brown (not/can/to believe) _____ it.

So the next night he (to try) _____ again and

then every night for a week, and each night the same thing (to happen)

_____.

Mr Brown (to be) _____ amazed and his wife (to be)

_____ amazed, too, that is, until she (to meet)

_____ Mrs Fry at a coffee morning one day.

Mrs Brown (just/to finish) _____ telling

the story when Mrs Fry said, "That's funny. My husband (to like)

_____ owls, too, and he (to go out)

_____ at 11 pm for months now to hoot to them as

well, but it (to be) _____ just last week that an owl

suddenly (to begin) _____ to hoot back at him."

	Das kann ich hier üben!	Das kann ich jetzt!	☺	😐	☹
Ich kann die *present and future tenses* richtig verwenden.			☐	☐	☐
Ich kann die *past and past perfect tenses* richtig verwenden			☐	☐	☐

Das Gerundium *(gerund)*

Das kann ich hier üben!   Das kann ich jetzt!

- ❑ Die Bildung des Gerundiums
- ❑ Die Verwendung des Gerundiums als Subjekt
- ❑ Die Verwendung als Objekt nach bestimmten Verben
- ❑ Die Verwendung als Objekt nach bestimmten Verbindungen aus Verb/Adjektiv/Nomen + Präposition
- ❑ Grundlegendes zum Objekt vor dem Gerundium
- ❑ Die Verwendung als Objekt nach bestimmten Ausdrücken
- ❑ Die Verwendung als Objekt nach bestimmten Konjunktionen

Bildung
Das ist wichtig!

Unter dem Gerundium versteht man die **Kombination Verb + -ing**, z. B. *working, running, tidying* usw. Es sieht aus wie der *-ing*-Teil des *present progressive* (ohne *I am, you are, he is* usw.). Das Gerundium kannst du als **Subjekt oder** als **Objekt** des Satzes verwenden.

Verwendung des Gerundiums – Teil 1
Das ist wichtig!

Das Gerundium kann als Subjekt oder als Objekt des Satzes dienen. Als **Subjekt** des Satzes steht es **an erster Stelle**:

(Das) Laufen ist gesund.
Walking is good for you.

Übung 1

Complete these sentences using the gerund.

1 *(Zur Schule zu laufen)* is good for you.

_____ is good for you.

2 *(Das Einkaufen in New York)* is really great, but …

_____ is really great, but …

Verwendung des Gerundiums – Teil 1

3 ... *(das Autofahren in der Stadt)* is a nightmare¹.

   ... _____ is a nightmare.

4 *(Mein Zimmer aufzuräumen)* isn't one of my hobbies.

   _____ isn't one of my hobbies.

5 *(Den ganzen Tag zu Hause zu sitzen)* is terribly boring.

   _____ is terribly boring.

Übung 2

These are Lily's plans for next week. She has eight hobbies. What are they?

On Monday Lily's friend Charlotte is coming round to her house and they are going to watch a DVD together. After that they want to play some games on the Wii. Charlotte has promised to bring her new Harry Potter book because Lily hasn't read that yet.

On Tuesday Lily is going to the youth club to play table-tennis with Sophie. On Wednesday Sophie has invited her round to her house. They are going to listen to her new CDs.

On Thursday there is a good film on TV, so Lily is going to stay at home and watch that. On Friday she has arranged to go shopping with Katie in the afternoon, and then in the evening they are going to go to the cinema together.

Lily's hobbies are watching DVDs,

_____ _____

_____ _____

_____ _____

and _____

And what are your hobbies?

---
1 *nightmare* = Albtraum

Das Gerundium *(gerund)*

Verwendung des Gerundiums – Teil 2

Das ist wichtig!

Als **Objekt** des Satzes steht das *gerund* (Verb + *-ing*)
1. nach bestimmten **Verben** (*to like, to love, to enjoy, …*)
2. nach bestimmen **Verbindungen** aus **Verb/Adjektiv/Nomen + Präposition** (*in, at, on, about, …*)
3. nach bestimmten **Ausdrücken** (*it's no use, …*)
4. nach **Konjunktionen** (*after, before, without, …*)

Das *gerund* nach bestimmten Verben

Das ist wichtig!

Verben, die das *gerund* verlangen, sind unter anderem:
to like, to love, to enjoy, to hate, can't stand, to imagine, to risk, to mind, to finish, to keep, to stop

Ich hasse es, früh aufstehen zu müssen.
I **hate having** to get up early.

Übung 3

Rewrite these sentences so that they mean the same as the original sentence. But this time use a verb plus gerund construction.

> **TIPP**
>
> Das *gerund* steht direkt hinter dem ersten Verb (das Wort *it* fällt weg!).

1. Emily hates it when she is ill.

   Emily _hates being_ ill.

2. My dad learned Latin when he was at school, but he didn't like it.

   My dad _____ Latin when he was at school.

3. Luke loves it when he is the centre of attention[2].

   Luke _____

4. What do you do in your free time? What do you enjoy?

   _____

---
2 *to be the centre of attention* = im Mittelpunkt stehen

Das *gerund* nach bestimmten Verben

5   Would you like to live in New York? Could you ever imagine it?

    _____

6   Could you wait for me? Would you mind?

    _____

7   That phone is ringing again. It never stops.

    _____

Übung 4

Complete these sentences with one verb from line A and one verb from line B. Remember to use the gerund for the second verb. Mind the tenses.

A: to finish – to mind – to keep – to risk – to enjoy – to miss
B: to catch – to be – to try – to get – to read – to show

1   When Ben moves to New York, he won't miss his teachers, but he
    _____ with his friends.

2   Amy decided to do her homework because she didn't want to
    _____ into trouble again.

3   You needn't pick me up from the airport. I don't
    _____ the train.

4   Don't worry if you are not successful at first. Just
    _____ .

5   I gave the magazine to Amy because I
    _____ it.

6   When Katie's cousin comes to stay with her in New York, she
    _____ her around the city.

Das Gerundium *(gerund)*

Das *gerund* nach Verb-Präposition-Verbindungen

Das ist wichtig!
Verb-Präposition-Verbindungen, die das *gerund* verlangen, sind unter anderen:
to look forward to, to believe in, to dream of, to feel like, to think of, to talk about, to care about, to worry about

Übung 5

Complete these sentences with the correct preposition + gerund.

1 We are thinking (to go) __of going__ to Florida for our holidays.

2 Sophie is looking forward (to move) _____ to France soon.

3 Do your best and don't worry (to make) _____ mistakes.

4 A lot of teenagers dream (to become) _____ famous.

5 I don't feel (to go) _____ out this evening.

6 The girls talked (to audition) _____ for a talent show.

7 Tom was lazy. He never believed (to work) _____ hard.

8 Ben didn't care (to lose) _____ the tennis match.

Das *gerund* nach Adjektiv-Präposition-Verbindungen

Das ist wichtig!
Adjektiv-Präposition-Verbindungen, die das *gerund* verlangen, sind unter anderen:
good at, bad at, tired of, interested in, afraid of, angry about, famous for, worried about, crazy about, used to

Übung 6

Complete these sentences with the correct preposition + gerund.

1 Sophie is very good (to play) __at playing__ the violin.

2 Claudia isn't afraid (to be) _____ in the house on her own.

3 Jack's mother is tired (to ask) _____ him to tidy his room.

Das *gerund* nach Adjektiv-Präposition-Verbindungen

4 I'm very bad (to sing) _____.

5 Are you worried (to go) _____ to the dentist's tomorrow?

6 I'm not crazy (to ski) _____.

7 Tom has never been interested (to play) _____ football.

8 We aren't used (to get up) _____ early on Sundays.

9 Some people are just famous (to be) _____ famous.

10 Ben was angry (to be dropped) _____ from the football team.

Übung 7

Complete these sentences with an expression from the box. Mind the tenses.

> not/to be good at – to be tired of – not/to be interested in –
> to be afraid of – to be worried about

1 Jenny didn't want to play the game again because she
   _was tired of_____ losing.

2 Don't tell Kate. She _____ keeping secrets.

3 Tom wants to leave now. He _____ missing his flight.

4 Why can you never be on time? I _____ having to wait for you all the time.

5 I didn't say anything because I _____ hurting his feelings.

6 Most teenagers today _____ learning more about how to protect the environment.

7 Don't become a teacher if you _____ working with children.

Das Gerundium (gerund)

Das *gerund* nach Nomen-Präposition-Verbindungen

Das ist wichtig!

Nomen-Präposition-Verbindungen, die das *gerund* verlangen, sind unter anderen:
the idea of, in danger of, chance(s) of, the reason for, the thought of, (dis)advantage of, experience of, (in the) hope of

Übung 8

Rewrite these sentences using a noun + preposition + gerund construction.

1. Kate didn't want to see Tim at the party. She couldn't bear the thought of it.

   Kate couldn't bear the _thought of seeing_ Tim at the party.

2. Do you think that we will win the World Cup? What are our chances?

   What are our chances _____?

3. Have you worked with children before? Do you have any experience?

   Do you have any _____?

4. Many immigrants went to America because they hoped to lead a better life.

   Many immigrants went to America _____

   _____.

Übung 9

Fill in a suitable noun + preposition.

1. I'm afraid there isn't much _____ finding the little girl alive.

2. The _____ living close to your school is that you don't have to get up early in the morning.

3. The _____ having games lessons at school is so that children get some exercise.

4. The _____ having to sing in front of an audience of millions filled me with fear.

Das Objekt vor dem *gerund*

Das ist wichtig!

Schau dir dieses Beispiel an:

Meine Mutter mag es nicht, wenn ich allein reise.
My mother doesn't **like** me travelling on my own.

> **! Merke**
> 1. Nach Verben, die das *gerund* verlangen, ist im Englischen eine Hauptsatz-Nebensatz-Konstruktion wie im Deutschen **nicht möglich**.
> 2. Die Wortstellung lautet: Subjekt – Verb – Objekt – *gerund*.
> 3. Vor dem *gerund* steht ein mögliches Personalpronomen immer in der Objektform (*me, you, her, him, it, us* oder *them*).

Übung 10

Rewrite these sentences using an object + gerund construction.

1. Mum hates it when we are late.

    Mum hates _us being late_____.

2. They lied to me. I can't stand that.

    I can't stand _____.

3. You can borrow my mobile. I don't mind.

    I don't mind _____.

4. Ben is coming home for Christmas. His mother is looking forward to that.

    Ben's mother _____
    _____.

5. My mother is always nervous when I go out on my own at night.

    My mother is always _____
    _____.

6. Sarah can speak three languages fluently. Her mother is very proud of this.

    Sarah's mother _____
    _____.

Das Gerundium (gerund)

Das *gerund* nach bestimmten Ausdrücken

Das ist wichtig!

Bestimmte **Ausdrücke**, die das *gerund* verlangen, sind unter anderen:	
How about	Wie wäre es, wenn wir spazieren gehen?
What about	**How about *going* for a walk?**
It's no good/use	Es hat keinen Zweck/Sinn, auf ihn zu warten.
	It's no use *waiting* for him.
It's (not) worth	Der Film war nicht gut. Es lohnte sich nicht, ihn anzuschauen.
	The film wasn't good. It wasn't worth *watching*.
There's no point in	Es hatte keinen Zweck/Sinn, ihn anzurufen.
	There was no point in *calling* him.

Übung 11

Finish these sentences using the words in brackets.

1. *(es hat keinen Sinn/to apologize)* There <u>is no point in apologizing</u> if you don't mean it.

2. The book is really interesting. *(es lohnt sich/to read)*

   _____.

3. The weather is so nice. *(wie wäre es wenn, wir/to go for a walk)*

   _____?

4. The computer was so old that *(es lohnte sich nicht/to repair)*

   _____.

5. The matter was so unimportant that *(es hatte keinen Zweck/to talk about)* there _____ it.

6. *(es hat keinen Zweck/to offer)* It _____

   him advice. He never listens anyway.

7. *(es hat keinen Zweck/to offer)* There _____

   him advice. He never listens anyway.

Das *gerund* nach Konjunktionen

Das ist wichtig!

...without + gerund.

...phone him.

...stop for lunch.

7 The film star waved to the crowd. Then she drove away in a large black car.

Das Gerundium *(gerund)*

Übung 13

Complete the text using a verb + gerund construction. Mind the tenses.

> keep/do – enjoy/go – think of/dye – not to mind/go – feel like/get – keep/make fun of – start/laugh – start/bully – stop/worry (2x) – keep/call

Amy's Diary

Dear Diary,

They did it again. They all laughed at me again in class. Tim wrote some stupid story about a girl with red hair, and then everybody looked at me and *(fingen an zu lachen)* _____.

(Warum machen sie das immer wieder) Why _____

_____ that? *(Warum machen sie sich immer über meine roten Haare lustig)* Why _____ my red hair?
(Warum müssen sie mich immer wieder Ginger[3] nennen)

Why _____ me Ginger? My name is Amy, not Ginger!
There was a time when *(es mir eigentlich Spaß gemacht hat, in die Schule zu gehen)* I actually _____ to school.
Well, maybe not exactly enjoy, but at least *(hat es mir nichts ausgemacht, in die Schule zu gehen)* I _____ to school. But not now. Not since that horrible Tim joined the class and *(fing an, mich zu mobben)* _____ me.
Most days *(habe ich nicht mal Lust, aus dem Bett herauszukommen)* I

_____ even _____ out of bed. Mum says *(ich solle aufhören, mir Sorgen zu machen)* I _____

_____ about stupid people like Tim. But that's easy to say, isn't it?

---
[3] *Ginger* = Rotschopf

Das *gerund* nach Konjunktionen

(Wie kann ich aufhören, mir Sorgen zu machen) How _____

_____ when he makes my life such hell? *(Ich habe sogar

schon daran gedacht, mir die Haare schwarz färben zu lassen)* I _____

even _____ my hair black. But Mum says if I

do that, then the bullies will win.

Dear Diary, help me, please!

		☺	😐	☹
Das kann ich hier üben!	**Das kann ich jetzt!**			
Ich beherrsche die Bildung des Gerundiums.		☐	☐	☐
Mit der Verwendung des Gerundiums als Subjekt kenne ich mich aus.		☐	☐	☐
Ich kenne die wichtigsten Verben, die das Gerundium als Objekt verlangen.		☐	☐	☐
Mir sind die wichtigsten Verbindungen aus Verb/Adjektiv/Nomen + Präposition geläufig, nach denen das Gerundium als Objekt stehen muss.		☐	☐	☐
Ich habe Grundlegendes zum Objekt vor dem Gerundium verstanden.		☐	☐	☐
Ich kenne die wichtigsten Ausdrücke und Konjunktionen, die das Gerundium als Objekt verlangen.		☐	☐	☐

Der Infinitiv

| Das kann ich hier üben! | Das kann ich jetzt! |

- ❏ Den Infinitiv mit *to* nach Fragewörtern
- ❏ Den Infinitiv mit *to* anstelle eines Relativsatzes
- ❏ Den Infinitiv zum Ausdruck einer Absicht
- ❏ Den Infinitiv mit *to* nach Adjektiven
- ❏ Den Infinitiv mit *to* nach bestimmten Verben

Die Verwendung des Infinitivs
Das ist wichtig!

Der Infinitiv (mit *to*) wird verwendet:
1. nach **Fragewörtern** (*what, where, how, …*),
2. **anstelle** eines **Relativsatzes**,
3. um eine **Absicht** auszudrücken (um … zu),
4. nach **Adjektiven** und deren **Steigerungen**,
5. nach bestimmten **Verben**.

Der Infinitiv mit *to* nach Fragewörtern
Das ist wichtig!

Nach bestimmten **Verben** wie
  to know (wissen), *to wonder* (sich fragen), *to be sure* (sich sicher sein), *to show* (zeigen), *to have an idea/no idea* (eine/keine Ahnung haben), *to decide* (sich entscheiden) usw.
+ **Fragewörtern** wie
  when, where, what, which, how much, how many, whether (ob) usw.
kannst du, statt eines Nebensatzes, eine Infinitivkonstruktion verwenden:

1. Kannst du mir zeigen, wo ich hingehen soll?
   Can you show me **where to go**?
2. Wir sind uns nicht sicher, ob wir Tim einladen sollen oder nicht.
   We aren't sure **whether to invite** Tim or not.

!**Merke**

Bei einer **Infinitivkonstruktion** steht *whether* (ob) anstelle von *if*.

Der Infinitiv mit *to* nach Fragewörtern

Übung 1

Complete these sentences using an infinitive construction.

1. Mark doesn't know what he should do.

    Mark doesn't know _what_ _to do_ .

2. I don't know who I can ask.

    I don't know _____ _____.

3. Tom has no idea how he should behave.

    Tom has no idea _____ _____

4. The teacher showed the children where they had to go in an emergency.

    The teacher showed the children _____ _____ in an emergency.

5. Ellie isn't sure what she must do when she arrives in New York.

    Ellie isn't sure _____ _____ when she arrives in New York.

6. Daniel is wondering if she should buy a new mobile phone or not.

    Daniel is wondering _____ _____ a new mobile phone or not.

7. Amy isn't sure which trousers she should wear to the party.

    Amy isn't sure _____ trousers _____ to the party.

8. Daniel hasn't decided if he should go by bus or by train.

    Daniel hasn't decided _____ _____ by bus or by train.

Der Infinitiv

Übung 2

Daniel's mum gives him some jobs to do while she is out. When she comes back, she asks him about them. Complete Daniel's answers. Use a question word from the box and an infinitive construction.

> where – who – which – how – what

Mum: Daniel, did you <u>put</u> the clothes away?

Daniel: No, Mum. I didn't know <u>where</u>   <u>to put</u>   them.
Mum: Did you <u>clean</u> the windows?

Daniel: No, Mum. I wasn't sure _____ windows _____.
Mum: Did you <u>look</u> for the front door key that you lost yesterday?

Daniel: No, Mum. I didn't know _____ _____.
Mum: Did you <u>cook</u> the meal?

Daniel: Oh Mum! You know I don't know _____ _____.
Mum: Did you <u>record</u> my favourite programme?

Daniel: Sorry Mum. I wasn't sure _____ programme _____.
Mum: Well, did you <u>do</u> your Maths homework?

Daniel: No Mum. It was so difficult. I had no idea _____

_____ it.
Mum: Well, why didn't you <u>phone</u> someone and ask them to help you?

Daniel: I didn't know _____ _____.

Übung 3

Complete the text using infinitive constructions. Use a question word from the box:

> who – where – which – whether – how – what

and one of the following verbs:

> to ask – to wait – to get – to go (2x) – to do – to take

70

Der Infinitiv mit *to* nach Fragewörtern

Ben is in New York for the first time. There are so many sights to see that he doesn't know _where_ _to go_ first. He would like to go to the Empire State Building, but he has no idea _____ _____ there, so he has to ask somebody.

There are so many people on the street that at first he isn't sure _____ _____. A friendly woman in a red dress tells him that it is too far to walk and that he should take a cab or go by subway. Ben isn't sure _____ subway _____, so he decides to go by cab. When he arrives at the Empire State Building, there is a long queue outside, so now Ben doesn't know _____ _____ in the queue or _____ _____ somewhere else first. He is really unsure _____ _____.

Übung 4

Translation practice.

1. Ich wusste nicht, was ich sagen sollte.

2. Kate wusste, wen sie anrufen konnte.

3. Jack ist sich nicht sicher, was er tun soll.

4. Ich kann mich nicht entscheiden, welche Schuhe ich tragen soll.

5. Ich weiß nicht, wie man das auf Englisch sagt.

Der Infinitiv

Der Infinitiv mit *to* anstelle eines Relativsatzes

Das ist wichtig!

Anstelle eines **Relativsatzes** kannst du insbesondere nach
1 *the first/second/third* usw.,
2 *the next/last/only one* und
3 einer **zweiten Steigerungsform** (*the best thing, the most important thing*)
eine **Infinitiv-mit-*to*-Konstruktion** verwenden.

Übung 5

Look at the example. Then complete the other sentences in the same way.

1 Sir Edmund Hillary was <u>the first person who climbed</u> Mount Everest.

   Sir Edmund Hillary was __the first (person) to climb__ Mount Everest.

2 <u>The most sensible thing that you can do</u> is to say nothing at all.

   _____ is to say nothing at all.

3 Most pupils did well in the test, but Ben was <u>the only one who got an A</u>.

   Most pupils did well in the test, but Ben was

   _____.

4 Emily was <u>the last person who arrived</u> at the party.

   Emily was _____ at the party.

5 <u>The next person who talks</u> will be sent out of the classroom.

   _____ will be sent out of the classroom.

6 You are <u>the second person who has said that</u>.

   You are _____.

7 <u>The best thing you can do</u> is to keep quiet.

   _____ is to keep quiet.

Der Infinitiv zum Ausdruck einer Absicht

Das ist wichtig!

Wie im Deutschen kannst du im Englischen einen Infinitiv verwenden, um über eine **Absicht** zu berichten (um … zu).

Übung 6

Complete these sentences with a verb from the box.

> to protect – to ask – to celebrate – to think about – to invite

1 I can't answer your question right away. I need some time _____ it.

2 There are a lot of things you can do _____ the environment.

3 It's my dad's birthday today. We are going out this evening _____.

4 I stopped a man in the street _____ the way.

5 Ben phoned _____ me to the disco on Saturday.

Übung 7

Complete these sentences with your own ideas.

1 I went to the supermarket _____ some meat.

2 You will need a knife _____ the bread.

3 I went to the travel agency _____ some brochures.

4 It took Ben ages _____ his homework yesterday.

5 Nowadays you don't always need a special talent _____ a star.

6 You need to be creative _____ a good story.

Der Infinitiv

Der Infinitiv mit *to* nach Adjektiven

Das ist wichtig!

Nach *it is/it was/it will be* + **Adjektiven** wie *easy, difficult, good* usw. und ihren Steigerungsformen (*easier, easiest, more difficult, most difficult* usw.) steht meistens der Infinitiv:

It's too **hot to do** anything today.
It's best not to sit in the sun for too long.

Übung 8

Complete these sentences. Use one adjective and one verb from each box.

sorry – ~~better~~ – easy – best – quicker – difficult – dangerous – surprised

to hear – to read – to see – to swim – not to mention – to find – ~~not to invite~~ – to walk

1 If Jack comes to the party, there will be trouble. I think it would be

   better   _not to invite_   him.

2 The book was very entertaining and it was also very _____

   _____.

3 It's a very sensitive subject. I think it would probably be _____

   _____ it at all.

4 I was _____ _____ about your accident.

5 I think we ought to take the train into town. On Saturdays it is always so

   _____ _____ a place to park the car.

6 Let's not wait for the next bus. I'm sure it will be _____

   _____.

7 Is it _____ _____ in the sea at this time of year?

8 I was _____ _____ Jack at the party. I didn't think he would be there.

Der Infinitiv mit *to* nach bestimmten Verben – Teil 1

Das ist wichtig!

Den Infinitiv mit *to* wird (unter anderen) nach folgenden Verben verwendet:

vereinbaren	*to arrange*	schaffen	*to manage*
entscheiden	*to decide*	anbieten	*to offer*
vergessen	*to forget*	versprechen	*to promise*
hoffen	*to hope*	sich weigern	*to refuse*
lernen	*to learn*	versuchen	*to try*
scheinen	*to seem*	vorhaben	*to plan*
wollen	*to want*	… möchte/st/t/n	*… would like*

Übung 9

Complete the sentences with a verb from the box.

> to help – to go – to meet – to be – to buy – to explain – not to tell – to sail – to listen – to win – to answer

1. Olivia and Tom hadn't seen each other for a long time, so they arranged ___to meet___ that evening.

2. Amy couldn't understand the homework, so I offered _____ her.

3. What did you do on holiday? – I learned _____ .

4. Katie seems _____ quite happy at her new school.

5. Harry tried _____ why he had got home late, but his mother refused _____ .

6. Where are the biscuits, Mum? – Oh dear, I forgot _____ them.

7. The test was difficult but I managed _____ most of the questions.

8. We were all very tired, so we decided _____ to bed early.

9. Every week millions of people hope _____ the lottery.

10. Jack promised _____ anyone my secret.

Der Infinitiv

Übung 10

Complete these sentences with a verb from the box. Mind the tenses.

> to refuse – to want – to decide – to hope – to promise – to plan – to manage

1. I asked Lily where she had been, but she _____ to tell me.
2. My mother is going to phone my class tutor because she _____ to know how I am getting on at school now.
3. Hannah left for Scotland this morning. She _____ to phone me as soon as she arrived.
4. Amy hasn't tidied her room yet, but she definitely _____ to do it this afternoon.
5. To everyone's amazement Jack _____ to pass his driver's license yesterday.
6. I don't know the results of the test yet, but I _____ to get them soon.
7. Jenny _____ to join the Drama Club this year.

Übung 11

Complete these sentences with a verb from each of the boxes. Mind the tenses.

> to hope – to decide – to plan

> to start – to look for – to visit

1. Many immigrants went to America because they _____ _____ a better life there.
2. When we are in New York next week, of course we _____ _____ all the usual tourist attractions.
3. The apartment is too small for a family of four, so the Smiths _____ _____ a larger one.

Der Infinitiv mit *to* nach bestimmten Verben – Teil 2

Das ist wichtig!

Nach den Verben

erwarten	**to expect**	wollen	**to want**
befehlen	**to tell**	… möchte/st/t/n	**… would like**

kannst du

1 einen **Infinitiv mit *to*** oder
2 ein **Objekt** (*me, you, him, her, it, us, them*) + **to** + Infinitiv (aber **niemals** einen „dass"-Satz wie im Deutschen)

verwenden:

1 Jack **wants to buy** a new printer for his computer.
   Jack will sich einen neuen Drucker für seinen Computer kaufen.
2 He **would like his father (him) to lend** him the money for it.
   Er möchte, dass sein Vater (er) ihm das Geld dafür leiht.

Übung 12

Can you finish these sentences?

1 Amy wanted *(ihr Fahrrad verkaufen)* _____.

2 She wanted *(dass ich es verkaufe)* _____.

3 They would like *(in den Zoo gehen)* _____.

4 They would like *(dass wir mitgehen)* _____.

5 I didn't expect *(sie auf der Party zu sehen)*

   _____ at the party.

6 I didn't expect *(dass sie auf der Party sein würde)*

   _____ at the party.

7 Can you do your homework on your own or *(möchtest du, dass ich dir helfe)*

   _____?

Der Infinitiv

8 I didn't take an umbrella with me because I didn't expect *(dass es regnen würde)* _____ .

9 Ben didn't tell Jenny the truth because he didn't want *(dass sie weint)* _____ .

10 Have you understood the grammar or *(möchtest du, dass ich es dir noch mal erkläre)* _____ _____ ?

Der Infinitiv mit *to* nach bestimmten Verben – Teil 3

Das ist wichtig!

Nach diesen Verben folgt **immer Objekt** (*me, you, him, her, it, us, them*) **+ to + Infinitiv**:

raten	*to advise*	erinnern	*to remind*
(ab)raten	*to advise somebody (not) to*	beibringen	*to teach*
einladen	*to invite*	warnen	*to warn somebody not to*

Ich riet ihm davon ab, seine Eltern anzulügen.
I advised him not to lie to his parents.

Übung 13

Finish these sentences so that they mean the same as the first sentence.

1 Mum to Jack: "Don't forget to buy some bread from the baker's."

   Jack's mother _reminded him to buy_____ some bread from the baker's.

2 Tom to you: "Would you like to go to the disco with me?"

   Tom _____ to the disco with him.

3 Dad to Katie and Lily: "Don't be late for school again!"

   Katie and Lily's dad _____ late for school again.

4 Mum to James: "If I were you, I would go to bed early."

James' mum _____ to bed early.

5 Mum to James: "If I were you, I wouldn't go to bed too late."

James' mum _____ to bed too late.

Übung 14

Translation practice. Use an extra sheet.

1 Das beste ist früh am Morgen loszufahren. *(It's … leave …)*
2 Mit dem Auto zu fahren ist billiger. *(It's …)*
3 Jenny war die erste, die ankam.
4 Wer hat den Raum als Letzter verlassen?
5 Ich brauche etwas Zeit, um darüber nachzudenken.
6 Sie rieten ihm, einige Wochen in einer Schule in England zu verbringen.
7 Sie wollen, dass wir ihnen etwas Geld leihen.
8 Wir haben sie gewarnt, das Wasser nicht zu trinken.

Das kann ich hier üben!	Das kann ich jetzt!			
		☺	😐	☹
Ich beherrsche die Verwendung des Infinitivs mit *to* nach Fragewörtern.		☐	☐	☐
Mit der Verwendung des Infinitivs mit *to* anstelle eines Relativsatzes kenne ich mich aus.		☐	☐	☐
Ich weiß, wie man den Infinitiv verwendet, um eine Absicht auszudrücken.		☐	☐	☐
Ich beherrsche die Verwendung des Infinitivs mit *to* nach Adjektiven.		☐	☐	☐
Mir sind die wichtigsten Verben geläufig, nach denen der Infinitiv mit *to* steht.		☐	☐	☐

Gerundium oder Infinitiv?

Das kann ich hier üben! **Das kann ich jetzt!**

- ❏ Die Verwendung des Gerundiums und des Infinitivs
- ❏ Gerundium oder Infinitiv nach *chance*
- ❏ Bedeutungsunterschiede durch Verwendung des Gerundiums oder des Infinitivs

Die Verwendung des Gerundiums und des Infinitivs

Das ist wichtig!

Verwende das **Gerundium**
1. nach folgenden **Verben**: *to like, to love, to hate, to enjoy, to finish, to imagine, to miss, to risk, to start, to begin, can't stand*
2. nach **Verben + Präpositionen**: *to look forward to, to believe in, to dream of, to feel like, to keep (on), to think of, to talk about, to worry about, to care about*
3. nach **Adjektiven + Präpositionen**: *good at, bad at, tired of, interested in, afraid of, fond of, angry about, famous for, worried about, crazy about*
4. nach **Nomen + Präpositionen**: *the idea of, in danger of, chance(s) of, the reason for, the thought of, in the hope of*
5. nach *it's no use, it's (not) worth, how about*
6. nach *after, before, without*

Verwende den **Infinitiv**
1. nach folgenden **Verben**: *to arrange, to decide, to expect, to forget, to hope, to learn, to manage, to offer, to promise, to refuse, to start, to tell, to try, to want, to start, to begin, would like*
2. nach **Adjektiven**: *easy, difficult, hot, cold* usw.
3. um eine **Absicht** auszudrücken (um … zu)
4. nach *chance* (Gelegenheit)
5. nach **bestimmten Verben + Fragewörtern**: *what to do, where to go* usw.
6. **anstelle eines Relativsatzes**: *the first/last person to know, the man to ask* usw.

Übung 1

Complete the sentences with an infinitive or a gerund. Sometimes you will need to add a preposition.

1. I was surprised (to get) _____ Tom's e-mail this morning. I didn't expect (to hear) _____ from him so soon.

2. When I'm on holiday, I enjoy (to lie) _____ on the beach and (to do) _____ nothing at all.

3. Teenagers aren't always interested (to learn) _____ for school. Sometimes they have better things (to do) _____.

4. The children love (to live) _____ in the country. They say they wouldn't want (to live) _____ anywhere else. They certainly couldn't imagine (to live) _____ in a town.

5. Mum says she is very busy just now but she will be happy (to help) _____ you later.

6. Ben doesn't want (to go) _____ to tennis practice any more. He says he is tired (to play) _____ tennis.

7. The little girl fell into the pond and was in danger (to drown) _____.

8. (to eat) _____ too much junk food is bad for your health.

9. Tim is looking forward (to play) _____ football on Saturday.

10. Kate was so embarrassed she didn't know where (to look) _____.

11. Let's take the bus. It's too far (to walk) _____.

Gerundium oder Infinitiv?

Übung 2

Complete the sentences with an infinitive or a gerund. Sometimes you will need to add a preposition.

1. The thought (to have to) _____ stay in the house alone didn't frighten Kevin.

2. When she started at her new school, Sophie hoped (to make) _____ new friends very quickly.

3. Jim advised us (not/to drive) _____ through the city in the rush-hour.

4. If you are good (to read) _____ maps, you won't need a navigation system.

5. I decided (to stay) _____ at home last night because I didn't feel well.

6. Grandma says she would love (to visit) _____ us next week.

7. I told him that I wasn't interested (to go) _____ to the party with him, but he kept (to ask) _____ me.

8. Are you good (to learn) _____ languages?

9. I know I made a mistake but that really is no reason (to shout) _____ at me.

10. Jack promised (to be) _____ home before 6 o'clock.

Übung 3

Complete the sentences with an infinitive or a gerund. Sometimes you will need to add a preposition.

1. Have you decided where (to go) _____ for your holidays?

2. The band are talking (to tour) _____ the country next year.

3. I'm tired (to tell) _____ you not to make so much noise.

4 Jack won the race because he was the first (to cross) _____ the finishing line.

5 Do you enjoy (to live) _____ in a small village?

6 Ben left the house without (to say) _____ goodbye.

7 These suitcases are too heavy (to carry) _____.

8 Sophie's mother told her that (to go) _____ on a language course in the summer holidays would help improve her German.

9 Our new teacher finds it difficult (to remember) _____ our names.

10 Our new teacher has difficulty (to remember) _____ our names.

Das Gerundium oder der Infinitiv nach *chance*

Das ist wichtig!

Schau dir diese Beispiele an:

1 Will we have a **chance to visit** the museum?
 (= **Gelegenheit/Möglichkeit** haben, **etwas zu tun**)
2 What are the **chances of winning** the lottery?
 (= wie **wahrscheinlich** ist es, dass **etwas eintritt**?)

Übung 4

Complete these sentences with of + gerund or to + infinitive.

1 Our teacher has been so busy lately that she hasn't had a chance (to correct) _____ our last tests yet.

2 Is there any chance (to get) _____ tickets for the concert tonight?

3 There is no chance (to catch) _____ our train now. It leaves in 5 minutes.

4 If you had the chance (to travel) _____ anywhere in the world, where would you go?

Gerundium oder Infinitiv?

Übung 5

Fill in the gaps with an infinitive or a gerund. Sometimes you will need to add a preposition.

Would you like to be a celebrity?

In the past, celebrities were people who had become famous because they were exceptionally good (1 to do) something like (2 to sing), (3 to act) or (4 to play) a particular sport. Today, however, (5 to have) a special talent no longer seems (6 to be) a requirement[1] and anyone can become a star. Nowadays just (7 to have) a charismatic personality, (8 to be able to) pose in front of a camera, or simply (9 to be) a WAG (the glamourous wife or girlfriend of a famous footballer) are apparently all the qualifications you need.

So it is hardly surprising that many teenagers now seem (10 to believe) that even without any particular talent they still have a real chance (11 to become) a star. Thanks to the explosion of TV talent shows, teen magazines and websites such as YouTube and MySpace, for today's teenager the idea (12 to want/to be) a celebrity is no longer an impossible dream. The problem today is: Is this dream really still worth (13 to live)? My opinion is that it is not. Most teenagers associate (14 to be) famous with (15 to have) money, popularity, success and happiness. When they are asked their reasons (16 to want/to become) celebrities, they usually mention the money, freebies[2] and the admiration[3] of the fans. For them (17 to be) a celebrity seems such an exciting life. But what they do not realize is that where there are advantages, there are always disadvantages, too. Of course it must be great (18 to be) rich and famous, but remember that today (19 to become) famous is much easier

---

1   *requirement* = Bedingung
2   *freebies (free gifts)* = Werbegeschenke
3   *admiration* = Bewunderung

Das Gerundium oder der Infinitiv nach *chance*

than (20 to stay) famous. Once you are a celebrity you are under constant pressure (21 to perform) and (22 to impress[4]) people. Of course money will give you security[5], but will it bring you happiness? If it does, then why do so many celebrities take drugs?

Of course it must be wonderful (23 to be) so popular, but how will you know who your true friends are and who you can really trust? Of course it must be fantastic (24 to see) yourself on the front cover of glossy magazines, but what if they start (25 to write) stories about you that you don't want other people (26 to hear)? And what if they write lies about you? Of course it must be fun when people stop you in the street (27 to ask) you for your autograph, (28 to take) a photo of you on their mobile phone or just (29 to say) hello. But what if they start (30 to stalk) you? As a celebrity, your life is no longer your own. Would you like (31 to live) in a goldfish bowl? – I wouldn't.

(32 to be) rich and famous may sound great fun, but in reality (33 to be) a celebrity isn't always the glamourous life that people think it is. I would advise anybody (34 to think) very carefully before (35 to follow) this dream.

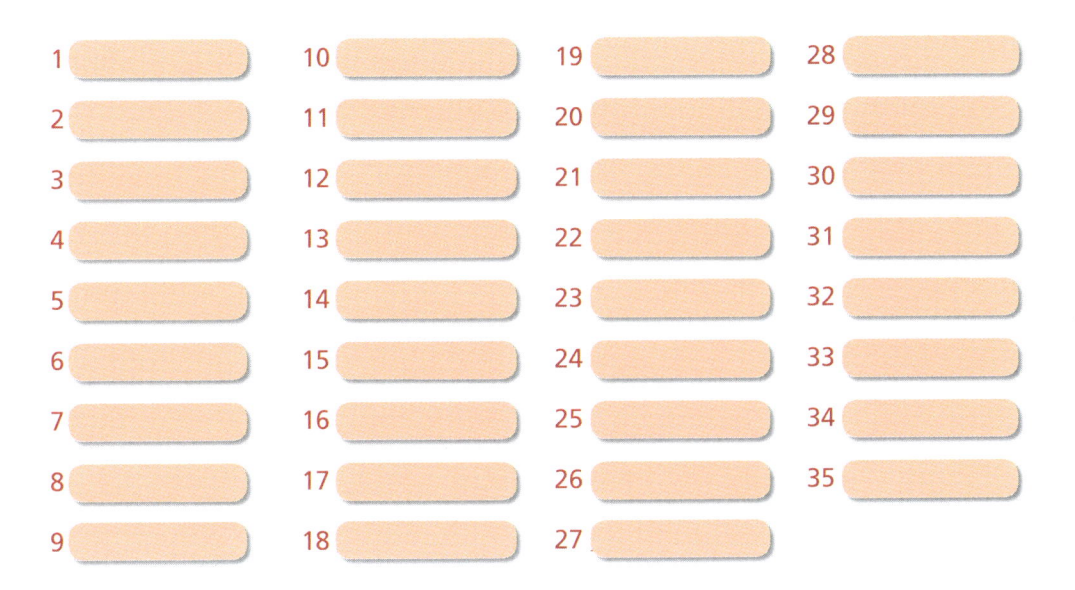

1.
2.
3.
4.
5.
6.
7.
8.
9.
10.
11.
12.
13.
14.
15.
16.
17.
18.
19.
20.
21.
22.
23.
24.
25.
26.
27.
28.
29.
30.
31.
32.
33.
34.
35.

---

4   *to impress* = beeindrucken
5   *security* = Sicherheit

Gerundium oder Infinitiv?

Bedeutungsunterschiede durch Verwendung des Gerundiums oder des Infinitivs

Das ist wichtig!

Nach *to stop, to go on, to mean, to try, to remember* und *to forget* hängt die **Bedeutung** des Verbs davon ab, ob ihm ein **Gerundium** oder ein **Infinitiv** folgt.

Verb	Bedeutung	Beispiel
to stop		
+ *gerund*	aufhören	Hör auf mich zu fragen! *Stop **asking** me!*
+ *infinitive*	anhalten, um etwas anderes zu tun	Ich hielt an, um nach dem Weg zu fragen. *I stopped **to ask** the way.*
to go on		
+ *gerund*	mit dem gleichen weitermachen	Er redete immer weiter. *He went on **talking**.*
+ *infinitive*	etwas anschließend machen	Anschließend sagte er … *He went on **to say** …*
to mean		
+ *gerund*	bedeuten	Das bedeutet, dass man früh aufstehen muss. *That means **getting** up early.*
+ *infinitive*	die Absicht haben, wollen	Ich wollte dich anrufen, aber … *I meant **to phone** you, but …*
to try		
+ *gerund*	etwas ausprobieren	Probiere es mit einem Messer. *Try **using** a knife.*
+ *infinitive*	versuchen	Versuche bitte zu erklären, … *Please try **to explain** …*
to remember		
+ *gerund*	sich erinnern	Ich erinnere mich, das Fenster geschlossen zu haben. *I remember **closing** the window.*
+ *infinitive*	daran denken	Denk daran, das Fenster zu schließen. *Remember **to close** the window.*
to forget		
+ *gerund*	vergessen	Ich werde nie vergessen, wie ich sie live gesehen habe. *I'll never forget **seeing** her live.*
+ *infinitive*	vergessen	Vergiss nicht, das Licht auszumachen. *Don't forget **to switch** the light **off**.*

Bedeutungsunterschiede durch Verwendung des Gerundiums oder des Infinitivs

Übung 6

Fill in the right form of the verb: gerund or infinitive?

1. Tom tried (to explain) _____ but his father wouldn't listen.
2. I have stopped (to buy) _____ those biscuits because they are too expensive.
3. Did you remember (to take) _____ the bottles to the bottle bank?
4. James tried (to follow) _____ his father into the music business, but with little success.
5. I didn't have a map, so I had to stop (to ask) _____ someone the way.
6. I remember (to meet) _____ him once before, but I can't remember where.
7. After Ben had finished school, he went on (to study) _____ at university.
8. The shop assistant ignored me completely and went on (to talk) _____ to her friend.
9. People often try (to rip off) _____ tourists. You have to be so careful.
10. I'm sorry. I didn't mean (to be) _____ rude.
11. Did you remember (to post) _____ the letter which was on the hall table? – I don't remember you (to ask) _____ me to do that.
12. Ben's dad accepted the job in Holland, even though it meant (only/to be able to) _____ see his family at weekends.
14. Mr Davis could get a job with an oil company, but that would mean (to move) _____ to Texas.
15. The teacher stopped (to think) _____ before (to answer) _____ the question.

87

Gerundium oder Infinitiv?

Übung 7

Fill in the right form of the verb: gerund or infinitive?

1 As soon as I realized that he was in trouble, I tried (to help) _____ him.

2 I remember (to hear) _____ Tom say that he would be on holiday in August.

3 We tried (to get) _____ tickets for the concert, but they were all sold out.

4 If you can't hear the TV, why don't you try (to turn) _____ up the volume ?

5 I've got a terrible headache. Please stop (to make) _____ such a noise.

6 You didn't forget (to buy) _____ the milk, did you?

7 I'm very busy. Please stop (to disturb) _____ me.

8 I'll never forget (to be stung) _____ by an angry wasp in the garden.

9 If you want to join the orchestra, that will mean (to practise) _____ the cello every day.

10 Don't forget (to do) _____ your homework, will you?

11 When new immigrants first arrive in Britain, they often only mean (to stay) _____ until they have earned enough money to go back home.

12 Tim wanted (to watch) _____ TV, but Kate wouldn't stop (to talk) _____ .

13 Did you remember (to take) _____ your medicine this morning?

14 First Tom worked as a waiter. Then he went on (to become) _____ the manager of the restaurant.

15 Why don't you stop (to worry) _____ about the test and start (to learn) _____ for it instead?

Bedeutungsunterschiede durch Verwendung des Gerundiums oder des Infinitivs

Übung 8

Translation practice. Use an extra sheet.

1. Ich wollte dich nicht verletzen. (*to mean/to hurt*)
2. Hör auf, mich zu ärgern! (*to stop/to annoy*)
3. Danach erklärte er die Spielregeln. (*to go on/to explain*)
4. Wir hielten an, um den Ausblick zu genießen. (*to stop/to enjoy*)
5. Vergiss nicht, deine Kamera mitzubringen! (*to forget/to bring*)
6. Ich werde nie vergessen, wie ich die Band live gesehen habe. (*to forget/to see*)
7. Hast du daran gedacht, für mich zur Apotheke zu gehen? (*to remember/to go*)
8. Liebe bedeutet, sich niemals entschuldigen zu müssen. (*to mean/to have to*)
9. Ich kann mich nicht erinnern, ihr die Geschichte erzählt zu haben. (*to remember/to tell*)
10. Versuch mal, so viele Informationen wie möglich über die Indianer herauszufinden! (*to try/to find out*)
11. Ich bat ihn ruhig zu sein, aber er redete immer weiter. (*to go on/to talk*)
12. Wenn ich nicht zu Hause sein sollte, versuche mir eine SMS zu schicken. (*to try/to text*)

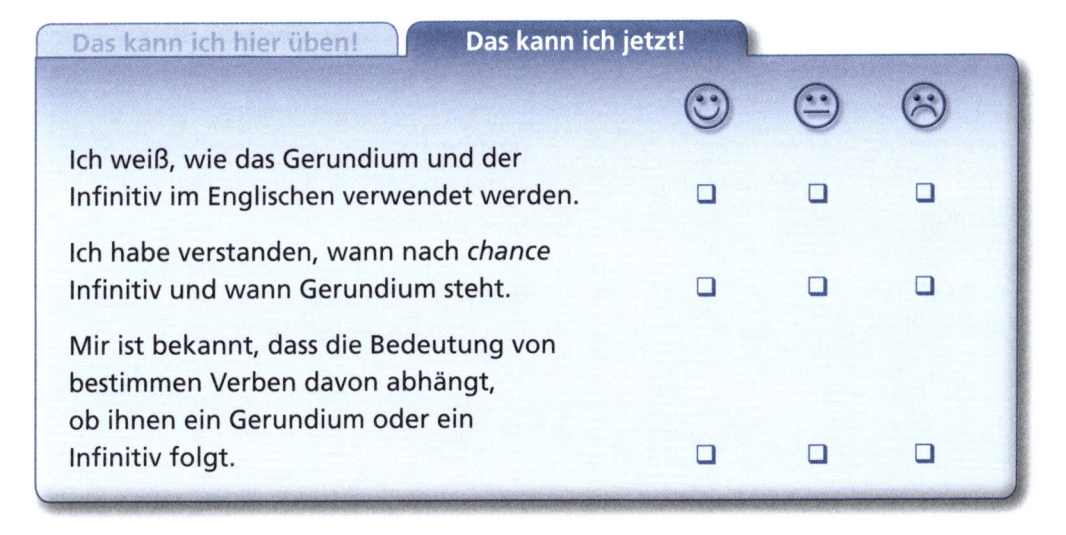

Das kann ich jetzt!

	☺	😐	☹
Ich weiß, wie das Gerundium und der Infinitiv im Englischen verwendet werden.	☐	☐	☐
Ich habe verstanden, wann nach *chance* Infinitiv und wann Gerundium steht.	☐	☐	☐
Mir ist bekannt, dass die Bedeutung von bestimmen Verben davon abhängt, ob ihnen ein Gerundium oder ein Infinitiv folgt.	☐	☐	☐

Die indirekte Rede

Das kann ich hier üben! **Das kann ich jetzt!**

- Verschiebung der Zeitformen bei der indirekten Rede
- Hilfsverben in der indirekten Rede
- Veränderung von Zeit- und Ortsangaben in der indirekten Rede
- Fragen in der indirekten Rede
- Aufforderungssätze in der indirekten Rede

Verschiebung der Zeitformen bei der indirekten Rede

Das ist wichtig!

Wenn das **einleitende Verb** im *simple past* steht, werden bei der Umformung der direkten in die indirekte Rede die **Verben** wie folgt **zurückgesetzt**:

Direkte Rede	Indirekte Rede
present	**past**
Jack to Ben: "**I'm** busy."	Jack **told** Ben (that) he **was** busy.
Jack: "**I'm doing** my homework."	Jack **said** he **was doing** his homework.
simple past	**past perfect**
Emily: "**I had** breakfast at 7.30."	Emily **said** she **had had** breakfast at 7.30.
present perfect	**past perfect**
Lily: "**I haven't been** well.	Lily **said** she **hadn't been** well and
I **have been coughing** all week."	she **had been coughing** all week.
past perfect	**past perfect**
Tom: "**I hadn't done** anything wrong."	Tom **said** he **hadn't done** anything wrong.
will future	**would + infinitive**
Ben: "**I'll be** 14 in June."	Ben **said** he **would** be 14 in June.

Verschiebung der Zeitformen bei der indirekten Rede

> **Merke**
> 1. Steht das **Einleitungsverb** im *simple past*, werden die Zeitformen wie folgt **verändert**:
>   present → past (2. Verbform)
>   past
>   present perfect } → past perfect (had + 3. Verbform)
>   past perfect
>   future (will) → conditional (would + Infinitiv)
> 2. Bei den Formen von **to be** werden folgende **Änderungen** vorgenommen:
>   am/is/are → was/were
>   was/were → had been

Übung 1

Put these sentences into indirect speech.

1. Amy to Ellie: "We usually go on holiday in August."

   Amy told Ellie (that) _____.

2. Tim: "I did my homework after lunch."

   Tim said (that) _____.

3. Jack to Ben: "I haven't seen Tom since Saturday."

   Jack _____.

4. Sophie: "I'll finish tidying my room after tea."

   Sophie _____.

5. Tom: "I took an aspirin because I wasn't feeling well."

   Tom _____
   _____.

6. Kate to her sister: "I'm tired because I have been working hard all day."

   Kate _____
   _____.

Die indirekte Rede

Hilfsverben in der indirekten Rede

Das ist wichtig!

Bei **Hilfsverben** werden folgende **Verschiebungen** vorgenommen:		
Direkte Rede	→	**Indirekte Rede**
can	→	could
may	→	might
must/have to/has to	→	had to
could	→	could
should	→	should
ought to	→	ought to
had to	→	had had to

Übung 2

Put these sentences into indirect speech. You only need to change the auxiliary verb.

1. Doctor to Jack: "You must stay in bed for a week."

   The doctor told Jack (that) _____.

2. Mum to Amy: "You should join a sports club."

   _____.

3. Sophie to Ellie: "I may be able to help you."

   _____.

4. Lucy: "We ought to take something to drink with us."

   _____.

5. Jack: "During the holidays I had to help my uncle on his farm."

   _____.

6. Ellie to her friends: "I'll tell you tomorrow if we can have the party at my house."

   _____.

Hilfsverben in der indirekten Rede

Übung 3

a) This is what the teacher told the children at the beginning of the lesson. Put it into indirect speech. You don't need a reporting verb at the beginning of every sentence. Use an extra sheet.

"We are going to practise a listening comprehension. You will hear the text twice. Before you listen to the text for the first time, you will have one minute to read the questions. You can start to make notes as soon as you have heard the text once. After you have heard the text for the second time, you must answer the questions in full sentences. The last time we did a listening comprehension, some of you only gave one-word answers. That's why you got a bad mark."

Begin like this: At the beginning of the lesson the teacher said … She told the children …

b) When Paris Hilton was interviewed about her celebrity status this is what she had to say. Put it into indirect speech. Use an extra sheet.

"People think that they know me, but they don't. They read stories in the media and think that is who I really am. But I'm not like my media image at all. I certainly don't consider myself to be a celebrity. In fact I hate the word. I'm a brand. I have my own perfume, my own make-up, shoes and hotels. I've starred on TV shows, in films and I've made a few records. There is nobody else quite like me. I don't really pay much attention to the media. People can think what they like. I'm living my life, I'm having the time of my life and I've never been happier. I didn't grow up wanting to be a celebrity. I wanted to be a vet because I love animals. But I am famous now, and I'm very proud of myself because I have achieved so much at such a young age. And that is all that matters to me."[1]

Begin like this: Paris Hilton said that people …

---

[1] Text nach: *"'People Think They Know Me'"*, Shout, Nr. 394, 27.4.2008, S. 21

Die indirekte Rede

Veränderung der Zeit- und Ortsangaben

Das ist wichtig!

Bei der Umformung der direkten in die indirekte Rede werden **Zeit- und Ortsangaben bei Bedarf** folgendermaßen **verändert**:

Direct speech		Indirect speech
today	→	that day (an jenem Tag)
tonight	→	that night (an jenem Abend)
this week	→	that week (in jener Woche)
tomorrow	→	the next/following day (am nächsten Tag)
next Tuesday	→	the next Tuesday
yesterday	→	the day before (am Tag zuvor)
two days ago	→	two days before (zwei Tage zuvor)
here	→	there
now	→	then

Übung 4

Put the sentences into indirect speech. Change the adverbs of place and time.

1 "I'm going to cook the lunch today," Lucy said.

   Lucy said _____.

2 "I'm sure Ellie will be here soon," Charles told Helen.

   Charles told Helen _____.

3 "I saw Mrs Dart the day before yesterday," Mrs Walker said.

   Mrs Walker said _____.

4 "No, I didn't do my homework yesterday," Chloe admitted.

   _____

   _____.

5 "I'll do it this evening," she promised.

   _____.

Veränderung der Zeit- und Ortsangaben

6 "I'm going to Paris next week," Mr Carter told his wife.

Mr Carter told his wife _____

_____.

7 "But you went there only a week ago," his wife complained.

His wife complained _____

_____.

8 "And you promised that I could come with you next time," she added.

_____

_____.

Übung 5

Fill in the correct adverb of time.

1 Tom: "I'm going to the cinema tonight".
   Lucy to Harry: "What did Tom say?"
   Harry: "He said that he is/was going to the cinema
   [tonight]." (tonight *bleibt unverändert, weil der Abend noch bevorsteht.*)

2 Kate to Amy on Monday: "I'm going to London next weekend."
   Amy to Emily on Tuesday: "Kate told me that she is/was going to London
   [   ]."

3 Tom to James: "I met Daniel yesterday."
   James to a friend (a month later): "When I last spoke to Tom about a month ago, he told me that he had met Daniel
   [   ]."

4 Lucy to her sister, Lily: "Katie is coming to see us tomorrow."
   Lily to Mum (later): "Lucy told me that Katie is/was coming to see us
   [   ]."

95

Die indirekte Rede

Fragen in der indirekten Rede

Das ist wichtig!

Direct question	Indirect question question word + subject + verb
Mrs A: "Where **is** Rakesh from?"	Mrs A <u>asked</u> **where** Rakesh **was** from.
Mum: "What **are** you **doing**, Ben?"	Mum <u>asked</u> Ben **what** he **was doing**.
Lisa: "How **do** you **get** to school?"	Lisa <u>wanted to know</u> **how I got** to school.
Mum: "**Did** you **sleep** well, Ben?"	Mum <u>asked</u> Ben **if** he **had slept** well.
Tim: "**Have** you **found** your key, Dan?"	Tim <u>asked</u> Dan **if he had found** his key.

> **! Merke**
>
> 1 Indirekte Fragesätze werden durch Verben wie *ask, wonder* oder *want to know* eingeleitet.
> 2 Die **Wortstellung** ist wie im Aussagesatz:
>   **einleitendes Verb + Fragewort + Subjekt + Verb + Objekt.**
> 3 **Umschreibungen** mit *do/does/did* fallen weg.
> 4 Beginnt die direkte Frage **nicht** mit einem **Fragewort** (*where, when, why, who* usw.), so wird die indirekte Frage durch *if* oder *whether* eingeleitet.

Übung 6

Put these questions into indirect speech.

1 "Ben and Ellie, why are you laughing?" the teacher asked.

   The teacher asked Ben and Ellie _____.

2 "How much pocket money do you get, Tim?" Dan wanted to know.

   Dan wanted to know _____.

3 "How long had you been waiting for the bus?" Ben asked his mother.

   Ben asked his mother _____.

4 "Will you be able to come to my party?" I asked Tom.

   I asked Tom _____.

Fragen in der indirekten Rede

5 "Where's your mother?" The shop assistant asked the little boy.

The shop assistant asked the little boy _____.

6 "How long have you been a fan of Coldplay, Tom?" Bill wanted to know.

Bill wanted to know _____.

7 "Would you like a cup of tea?" Mrs Bean asked her guest.

Mrs Bean asked her guest _____.

8 "Do you drink your tea with milk, Mr Jones?" Julia wanted to know.

Julia wanted to know _____.

9 "Who ate the biscuits?" Mum wondered.

Mum wondered _____.

Übung 7

These questions are in indirect speech. What did these people actually ask?

1 Ben wanted to know how much Jack had paid for the tickets.

Ben to Jack: "_____?"

2 The coach asked me why I hadn't been at football practice yesterday.

Coach: "_____?"

3 The teacher asked Ben what he wanted to do when he left school.

Teacher to Ben: "_____?"

4 Jack wanted to know if Ben had finished reading the magazine.

Jack: "_____?"

Die indirekte Rede

Aufforderungssätze in der indirekten Rede

Das ist wichtig!

Direct command/request	Indirect command/request person + (not) to + infinitive
Mum to Ben: "Please **take** the bottles to the bottle bank."	Mum <u>asked</u> **Ben to take** the bottles to the bottle bank.
"**Wait** for me outside the classroom," the teacher told the children.	The teacher <u>told</u> **the children to wait** for **him/her** outside the classroom.

!**Merke**

1. Indirekte Aufforderungssätze werden durch Verben wie *to ask* (bitten), *to invite, to tell, to warn, to advise* oder *to remind* eingeleitet.
2. Befehle und Aufforderungen in der indirekten Rede haben die **Wortstellung: einleitendes Verb + Person + *(not) to* + Infinitiv**.
3. Nach dem Einleitungsverb **folgt immer** ein **Personenobjekt** (Nomen oder Pronomen in der Objektform – *me, you, him, her, it, us, you, them*).

Übung 8

Put the following sentences into indirect speech.

1 to 4: Use one of the following introductory verbs:
to ask – to advise – ~~to remind~~ – to invite

1. "Don't forget to bring your CDs to the party, Harry."

   Emily _reminded Harry to bring his CDs to the party_.

2. "Could you pass me the sugar, please, Hannah?"

   Lily _____.

3. "Never give anyone your phone number or address when chatting online."

   Amy's dad _____

   _____.

4. Mrs Banks to her neighbour: "Please come in and have a cup of tea."

   Mrs Banks _____.

Aufforderungssätze in der indirekten Rede

5 to 8: Use one of the following introductory verbs:
to advise – to tell – to ask – to remind

5   "Tom, you'd better go and see the doctor as soon as possible."

Tom's dad _____

_____.

6   "Please can you pick me up from school, Mum?"

Jane _____.

7   "Don't forget to hand in your homework by 9 o'clock, children."

The teacher _____

_____.

8   "Tidy your room before your guests arrive, Lily, and don't forget to put your socks in the basket."

Mum _____

_____.

9 to 12: Use one of the following introductory verbs:
to warn – to order – to advise – to tell

9   "Don't touch the fence or you will get an electric shock, Tim."

James _____

_____.

10   "Mary, you mustn't see that boy again."

Mary's parents _____.

11   "Don't worry if you get a bad mark in the test."

Jack's mother _____

_____.

12   "Learn the rules for indirect speech if you want to do well in the test, children."

The teacher _____

_____.

Die indirekte Rede

Übung 9

These commands and requests are in indirect speech. What did these people actually say?

1. The teacher told the children to stop talking and to concentrate on the lesson.

   Teacher to the children: "_____."

2. Aunt Julia invited Freddy to come and stay with them whenever he liked.

   Aunt Julia to Freddy: "_____."

3. Peter's dad warned him to drive slowly and not to drink any alcohol.

   Dad to Peter: "_____."

4. Kate's mother asked her to lay the table for tea.

   Mum to Kate: "_____?"

5. The teacher advised the students not to miss classes or there would be trouble.

   Teacher to students: "_____!"

Übung 10

Sophie and her mother are talking about the holidays. Put this dialogue into indirect speech.

Sophie's mum: "What are you going to do when the holidays start next week?"

Sophie's mum asked her _____

_____.

Aufforderungssätze in der indirekten Rede

Sophie: "I may go to France with Emily or I may go to Italy with Tom. I haven't decided yet."

Sophie replied that _____

_____.

Mum: "Have you thought about looking for a holiday job?"

So her mother asked her _____

_____.

Sophie: "I have tried to find one, Mum, but there aren't any."

Sophie explained that _____.

Mum: "Dixons are looking for a shop assistant in August. I saw their advert in the newspaper yesterday."

So then her mum told her _____

_____.

Mum: "Why don't you ring them and ask if you can come for an interview."

She suggested _____.

Sophie: "Oh Mum. I don't want to work in August. I was looking forward to relaxing at home."

When Sophie replied _____

_____ …

Mum: "And I was looking forward to you earning your own pocket money. Call them or send them your application before it is too late!"

… her mother said that _____

_____.

Die indirekte Rede

Übung 11

Amy and Lily are talking about teen magazines. Put this dialogue into indirect speech. You don't need to use every word. Use an extra sheet.

Amy: "Have you seen the interview with Tom Cruise in 'Heaven' this week?"

Lily: "I don't read 'Heaven' any more. I changed to 'Glory' about a month ago because I think it's much better. It has more articles on celebs[2], great style tips and good advice. And what's more it has super freebies[3]. This week they are giving away a fantastic make-up bag. The only bad thing about it is the price. It costs two pounds fifty, which I think is quite expensive."

Amy: "'Glory' sounds like a really good magazine. Can I have a look at one of yours?"

Lily: "Yeah, sure. Come round to my house this afternoon and I'll lend you the magazine from last week. But please don't come before 4 o'clock because I won't be home until then."

Begin like this: Amy asked Lily …

Übung 12

Put the verbs into the correct tense. Think about the rules for indirect speech.

1 Ben said that he (to meet) _____ Kate outside the cinema that evening.

2 The teacher told the children that they (can/to start) _____ their homework as soon as they (to finish) _____ exercise 2.

3 Holly asked me what I (to look for) _____.

4 The man asked me what I (to want) _____.

---

2 *celebs* = Promis
3 *freebies* = Werbegeschenke

Aufforderungssätze in der indirekten Rede

5 Sophie said that she (to be) _____ hungry because she (not/to eat) _____ anything since breakfast.

6 Ben said that he (not/to sleep) _____ well because he (to be) _____ cold in the night.

7 Amy said that she (not/to know) _____ what I (to talk about) _____ .

8 Jack said that he (can/not/to go) _____ to school this week because he (to be) _____ ill.

9 Jack said that he (can/not/to go) _____ to school last week because he (to be) _____ ill.

	Das kann ich hier üben!	**Das kann ich jetzt!**	😊	😐	☹
Ich beherrsche die Verschiebung der Zeitformen bei der indirekten Rede.			☐	☐	☐
Ich weiß, welche Verschiebungen bei Hilfsverben vorgenommen werden.			☐	☐	☐
Die Veränderungen von Orts- und Zeitangaben in der indirekten Rede sind mir klar.			☐	☐	☐
Ich weiß, wie Fragen in der indirekten Rede gebildet werden.			☐	☐	☐
Ich weiß, wie Aufforderungssätze in der indirekten Rede gebildet werden.			☐	☐	☐

Das Passiv

> **Das kann ich hier üben!**   Das kann ich jetzt!
>
> ❏ Was das Passiv ist und was man damit ausdrücken kann
> ❏ Die Bildung des Passivs
> ❏ Die Verlaufsform des Passivs
> ❏ Das Passiv und die modalen Hilfsverben
> ❏ Den Infinitiv Passiv
> ❏ Die Umwandlung von Aktivsätzen in Passivsätze
> ❏ Die Umwandlung von Pronomen des Aktivsatzes in Passivsätzen
> ❏ Das Verhalten von Verb-Präposition-Verbindungen beim Übergang vom Aktiv ins Passiv
> ❏ *any*, *anyone*, *anything* und das Passiv
> ❏ Fragen im Passiv

Was ist das Passiv?

Das ist wichtig!

Mit dem Passiv sagst du, was **mit jemandem** oder **mit etwas passiert**. Wer oder was die Handlung ausführt ist dabei uninteressant und wird meistens weggelassen.

Das Frühstück wird ab 7.30 serviert.
Breakfast is served from 7.30.

Man gab mir eine Spritze.
I was given an injection.

> **! Merke**
>
> 1 In der **deutschen Sprache** wird das Passiv mit einer Form von „werden" + **Partizip Perfekt** (3. Verbform) gebildet.
> 2 In der **englischen Sprache** wird das Passiv mit einer Form von *to be* + *past participle* (3. Verbform) gebildet.
> 3 Ein **deutscher Aktivsatz** mit „man" wird im **Englischen** oft mit einem **Passivsatz** wiedergegeben.

Die Formen

Das ist wichtig!

Diese Formen solltest du können:

Zeitform	Aktiv	Passiv (Form von *to be* + *past participle*)
simple present	take/takes	am/are/is taken
simple past	asked	was/were asked
present perfect	have/has told	have/has been told
past perfect	had given	had been given
will future	will inform	will be informed
(be) going to future	are going to build	are going to be built
conditional I	would sell	would be sold
conditional II	would have bought	would have been bought

Übung 1

Change the active forms of the verbs into passive forms.

1. he gives — he is given
2. they teach — they _____
3. I paid — I _____
4. they built — they _____
5. he has caught — he _____
6. we hadn't asked — we _____
7. she will invite — she _____
8. they would steal — they _____
9. I would have sent — I _____
10. it keeps — it _____
11. they flew — they _____
12. they are going to sell — they _____

Das Passiv

Die Verlaufsform des Passivs

Das ist wichtig!

Zeitform	Aktiv	Passiv
present progressive	am/is/are teaching	am/is/are **being** taught
past progressive	was/were showing	was/were **being** shown

> **Merke**
> 1 Die **Verlaufsform** des Passivs existiert nur in der **Gegenwart** und in der **Vergangenheit**.
> 2 Sie wird mit einer Form von *to be* + *being* + Verb in der 3. Form gebildet.

Übung 2

Fill in the correct form of the verb. Use the present progressive passive.

A lot of building work (to do) _____ in the town at the moment. A new town centre (to develop)

_____ and new office blocks and car parks

(to build) _____. A new school (also/to

plan) _____ also _____.

Übung 3

Fill in the correct form of the verb. Use the past progressive passive.

When I got home yesterday, a lot of work (to do)

_____

on the house. A new carpet (to lay) _____
on the stairs, a new kitchen (to install)

_____, the living room walls (to paint)

_____ and new curtains (to put up)

_____ in my bedroom.

Das Passiv und die modalen Hilfsverben

Das ist wichtig!

Die **modalen Hilfsverben** (*can, could, must, should* usw.) **bleiben** im Passiv **unverändert**. Nur der **Infinitiv** wird in *be* + Verb in der 3. Form umgewandelt.

can give	→	can be given	could buy	→	could be bought
must take	→	must be taken	should say	→	should be said
may put	→	may be put	might tell	→	might be told
mustn't put	→	mustn't be put	ought to tell	→	ought to be told

Übung 4

Can you complete these school rules with the correct form of the passive?

1. School uniform (must/to wear) _____ during school hours.

2. Hair (should/to keep) _____ off the face.

3. Small ear-rings (may/to wear) _____ by girls, but not by boys.

4. If possible, children (shouldn't/to drive) _____ to school.

5. Bicycles (can/to leave) _____ in the stands provided.

6. Mobile phones (may/to bring) _____ to school but they (mustn't/to use) _____ in the classroom.

7. Classrooms (must/to tidy) _____ at the end of each school day.

8. No ball games (may/to play) _____ inside the school buildings.

9. Pupils who break the rules (may/to suspend[1]) _____ and in serious cases (might/even/to expel[2]) _____ even _____ .

---
1 *to suspend* = zeitweilig vom Unterricht ausschließen
2 *to expel* = von der Schule verweisen

Das Passiv

Der Infinitiv Passiv

Das ist wichtig!

Nach Verben wie *to want, to expect, to seem, to have to* usw. steht das **zweite Verb** im **Infinitiv Aktiv** oder im **Infinitiv Passiv**.

Infinitiv Aktiv	Infinitiv Passiv
Ich will die Wahrheit wissen.	Ich will, dass man mir die Wahrheit erzählt.
I want to know the truth.	I want **to be told** the truth.

!**Merke**

Der **Infinitiv Passiv** wird mit *to be* + Verb in der 3. Form gebildet.

Übung 5

Complete this text with the active or passive infinitive of the verb.

Why do so many young people want (to become) _____ celebrities? Ask them and you will hear all the usual reasons: They would like (to pay) _____ well for doing very little work, (to invite) _____ to glamourous parties, (to upgrade) _____ on planes and not least of all (to admire) _____ everywhere they go. Being a celebrity seems (to be) _____ such an exciting life. Of course, life is only like that for the very few, but can you expect young people (to believe) _____ that?

Übung 6

Mixed tenses. – Fill in the correct form of the verb. Decide if you need the active or passive voice.

1 Have you seen this photo? It (to take) _____ at Dan's party but I don't know who (to take) _____ it.

2 (Germany/to win) _____ the World Cup in 2006? – No, they (to beat) _____ in the semi-finals by Italy.

Der Infinitiv Passiv

3 The older children (usually/to walk) _____ to school but their baby brother (always/to drive) _____ to kindergarten.

4 (your neighbours' house/to sell) _____ _____ yet? – No, they (to try) _____ to sell it for about six months now so it's probably too expensive.

5 Why (you/to be born) _____ in South Africa? – Because my parents (to live) _____ there at the time.

6 We (cannot/to use) _____ the bathroom yesterday because a new shower (to install) _____.

7 When Mum came home, she (to get) _____ a lovely surprise. The living room (to tidy) _____, the meal (to cook) _____ and the table (to lay) _____.

8 If you (to leave) _____ your bike here, it (may/to steal) _____.

9 If you (to offer) _____ a lot of money to appear on a reality TV show and to make a fool of yourself, (you/to do) _____ it?

10 We (to be able to) _____ swim in the lake last summer if it (not/to pollute) _____ by the new factory.

11 Do you believe celebs when they tell you they don't want (to recognize) _____?

Das Passiv

Vom Aktiv ins Passiv

Das ist wichtig!

Um einen Satz vom Aktiv ins Passiv umzuwandeln, musst du wie folgt vorgehen:
1. Suche das **Objekt des Aktivsatzes** (es steht hinter dem Verb) und mach es zum **Subjekt des Passivsatzes**.
2. Wähle eine **Form von** *to be* in der **gleichen Zeitform** wie im Aktivsatz:

simple present	*am, is* oder *are*
present progressive	*is being* oder *are being*
simple past	*was* oder *were*
past progressive	*was being* oder *were being*
present perfect	*have been* oder *has been*
past perfect	*had been*
will future	*will be*
(be) going to future	*am/is/are going to be*

3. **Passe** die Form von *to be* **dem neuen Subjekt** an und **beachte** dabei **Singular** und **Plural**.
4. Setze das **Vollverb** des Aktivsatzes in das *past participle* (3. Verbform).
5. Ist das Subjekt des Aktivsatzes eine **unbestimmte Person** wie *we, they, people, you, someone* usw., **lässt** man es **im Passivsatz weg**.
6. Ist das Subjekt des Aktivsatzes eine **bestimmte Person oder Sache**, wird es **im Passivsatz** durch *by* **angeschlossen**.

> **!Merke**
>
> **Aktivsatz** und **Passivsatz** stehen in der **gleichen Zeitform**.

Übung 7

Change the following active sentences into passive sentences.

1 Thousands of people visit the safari park each year.

_____

It's popular because they don't keep the animals in cages there.

_____

2 They are turning the book into a film,

___

but they aren't releasing the film until next year.

___

3 An eleven-year-old singer impressed the judges of a talent show.

___

But in the end the little girl didn't win the competition.

___

4 The band were giving a concert to raise money for charity.

___

But they weren't organising the event.

___

5 They have just built a new football stadium in our town,

___

but they haven't opened it yet.

___

6 The burglars had broken a window,

___

but the noise hadn't woken the neighbours.

___

7 The Casting Director will invite 50 people to audition for a role in a daily soap.

___

Das Passiv

8 He won't tell the applicants immediately if they have got the part.

9 They are going to publish the story in tomorrow's newspaper,

but they aren't going to print it on the front page.

Objekt- und Subjektpronomen

Das ist wichtig!

Ist das **Objekt** des Aktivsatzes ein **Pronomen**, musst du die **Objektform** in die **Subjektform umwandeln**:

Objektform:	me	you	him	her	it	us	you	them
Subjektform:	I	you	he	she	it	we	you	they

Übung 8

Change the following active sentences into passive sentences.

1 Somebody will tell her what to do.

2 My grandparents are meeting me at the airport.

3 Did a guide show them around New York?

4 Nobody drove us to school this morning.

Verben mit Präpositionen

Das ist wichtig!

Bei *to look after, to send for, to break into, to throw away, to run over* usw. **gehören Verben und Präposition zusammen**. Die **Präposition** steht **immer hinter dem Verb**:

Aktivsatz: *Nobody had switched off the TV.*
Passivsatz: *The TV hadn't been **switched off**. (nobody ist eine Verneinung!)*

!Merke

Ein Passivsatz fängt **nie** mit einer Präposition an!

Übung 9

Change the following active sentences into passive sentences.

1 They have cut down the old trees.

   The old trees have been cut down.

2 Somebody broke into Jenny's flat last week.

3 Somebody has put up a notice on the board.

4 They are going to pull down the old houses.

5 A nanny looks after the children.

6 The noise didn't wake up the baby.

Das Passiv

7 He has made up his mind.

8 The teacher will hand out the worksheets at the beginning of the lesson.

9 Nobody had switched off the lights.

10 Why didn't they send for a doctor if the boy was so ill?

any, anyone, anything und das Passiv

Das ist wichtig!

Schau dir diese Beispiele an:

They don't grow **any** vegetables in the gardens.
No vegetables are grown in the gardens.
They did**n't** invite **anybody** to their house.
Nobody was invited to their house.
They have**n't** done **anything**.
Nothing has been done.
They will **never** do **anything** about it.
Nothing will **ever** be done about it.

> ! **Merke**
> 1 Aktivsatz: n't ... any/anybody/anything
>   → Passivsatz: no/nobody/nothing
> 2 Aktivsatz: **never** ... any/anyone/anything
>   → Passivsatz: no/no-one/nobody **+ ever**
> 3 Das Verb wird nach *no*, *nobody* und *nothing* **nicht** zusätzlich verneint.

any, anyone, anything und das Passiv

Übung 10

Change the following active sentences into passive sentences.

1 They won't ask any questions.

2 We haven't seen anybody in his shop for weeks.

3 They never invited anybody to their house.

4 We didn't give any information to the press.

5 I want to know why you aren't doing anything about the pollution in this town.

Übung 11 Modale Hilfsverben

Change the following active sentences into passive sentences.

1 You must send the birthday card today.

2 You can keep a rabbit in the house or in the garden.

3 Somebody ought to tell him the truth.

Das Passiv

4 You can't make the sandwiches the day before the party.

5 Must we tell Kate's parents about the party?

6 I think we should call the police.

7 You can't do anything to help him.

Übung 12 Fragen im Passiv

These questions are in the active voice. Rewrite them in the passive.

1 Do they teach you how to cook at your school?

2 Is the record company organizing the event?

3 Did they take them on a sightseeing tour of London?

4 Why aren't they going to build the new hospital?

5 Did you have to tell your parents about the fire?

6 Did they sell all the cakes at the fete?

7 Was anybody looking after the children?

8 When are they going to open the new road?

any, anyone, anything und das Passiv

9   Had you parked your car in a no-parking zone?

10 How often have I told you not to leave your shoes in front of the door?

11 Who wrote the song?

Übung 13 Vom Aktiv ins Passiv – *Mixed Tenses*

Change the following active sentences into passive sentences.

1   Nowadays they make a lot of films in Vancouver.

2   They aren't holding the competition this year.

3   They can't do the operation until next year.

4   Nobody was using the computers on the second floor.

5   You must hand in your homework before 9 am.

6   Nobody will laugh at you if you make a silly mistake.

7   They haven't put the toys away, they have left them on the floor.

8   Somebody will show you where to go.

Das Passiv

9 It was only a small fire. They didn't have to call the fire brigade.

10 Somebody had checked the oil and pumped up the tyres.

Übung 14 Translation practice

Translate the German sentences.

> **TIPP**
>
> Denk daran, dass ein deutscher Aktivsatz mit „man" im Englischen oft mit einem Passivsatz wiedergegeben wird.

1 In den meisten Ländern spricht man Englisch.

2 Eine neue Dusche wird gerade eingebaut.

3 Das Geld wurde in seiner Wohnung gefunden.

4 Jeden Morgen werden wir von dem Hund geweckt.

5 Das Mädchen musste sofort ins Krankenhaus gebracht werden.

6 Weißt du, wann Amerika entdeckt wurde?

7 Die Informationen werden morgen mit der Post geschickt.

8 Die Bücher können im Internet bestellt werden.

9 Wo wurden diese Fotos gemacht?

any, anyone, anything und das Passiv

10 Wann muss der Hund gefüttert werden?

___

11 Warum musste Tom eingeladen werden?

___

12 Wie oft hat man ihm gesagt, dass er die Fenster schließen muss, bevor er weggeht?

___

___

13 Ich will nicht, dass jemand mich erkennt.

___

Das kann ich hier üben!	**Das kann ich jetzt!**			
		☺	😐	☹
Ich weiß, was das Passiv ist und was ich mit ihm ausdrücken kann.		❑	❑	❑
Ich beherrsche die Bildung des Passivs.		❑	❑	❑
Die Verlaufsform des Passivs kann ich.		❑	❑	❑
Ich weiß, wie sich die modalen Hilfsverben bei der Bildung von Passivsätzen verhalten.		❑	❑	❑
Ich beherrsche die Bildung und Verwendung des Infinitiv Passiv.		❑	❑	❑
Ich kann Aktiv- in Passivsätze umwandeln.		❑	❑	❑
Die Umwandlung von Pronomen des Aktivsatzes in Passivsätzen beherrsche ich.		❑	❑	❑
Ich weiß, wie sich Verb-Präposition-Verbindungen beim Übergang vom Aktiv ins Passiv verhalten.		❑	❑	❑
Mit dem Thema „*any, anyone, anything* und Passiv" kenne ich mich aus.		❑	❑	❑
Ich beherrsche die Bildung von Fragen im Passiv.		❑	❑	❑

Nomen/*nouns*

Das kann ich hier üben! Das kann ich jetzt!

- ❑ Regelmäßige und unregelmäßige Pluralformen
- ❑ Nomen, die nur im Singular stehen
- ❑ Nomen, die nur im Plural stehen
- ❑ Die Verwendung von *some/a piece of/a pair of*
- ❑ Das Stützwort *one/ones*
- ❑ Den Genitiv

Regelmäßige und unregelmäßige Pluralformen

Das ist wichtig!

Bei den **meisten** Nomen wird der Plural durch **Anhängen von -s** gebildet, z. B. *one book, two books*.

Aber es gibt **Ausnahmen**:

1. **-y** nach einem **Konsonanten** wird zu **-ies**:
   country ➔ countr**ies**; celebrity ➔ celebrit**ies**

2. **-fe** wird meist zu **-ves**:
   wi**fe** ➔ wi**ves**; li**fe** ➔ li**ves**

3. Wenn das Nomen auf **-x** oder **-ch** endet, wird die Pluralform mit **-xes** oder **-ches** gebildet:
   box ➔ bo**xes**; watch ➔ wat**ches**

4. **-o** wird zu **-oes** (gilt nicht für *photo, biro, piano, radio, pro*, diese Wörter enden auf *-os*):
   pota**to** ➔ pota**toes**; toma**to** ➔ toma**toes**

5. **Sonderformen**:
man	➔	men	tooth	➔	teeth	sheep	➔ sheep
woman	➔	women	foot	➔	feet	fish	➔ fish
child	➔	children	mouse	➔	mice		
person	➔	people	goose	➔	geese		

Regelmäßige und unregelmäßige Pluralformen

Übung 1

Complete these sentences with the word in brackets (). Decide whether you need a singular or a plural noun.

1. The neighbours are so loud. They are always having (party) __parties__ .

2. This (box) _____ is too small. Aren't there any larger ones? – Look in the attic. You'll find some larger (box) _____ there.

3. Ben's got so many (book) _____ but nowhere to put them. He really needs a few more (shelf) _____ in his room.

4. Mum usually buys our (potato) _____, (tomato) _____ and (egg) _____ from the market.

5. Who took those (photo) _____ of me? They're terrible.

6. There were only three (person) _____ on the bus: two (woman) _____ and a small (child) _____.

7. Don't ask Jack to help you. He's got two left (hand) _____ and two left (foot) _____.

8. An argument essay is an essay in which you have to discuss the (pro and con) _____ of a particular subject.

9. Have you got a dishwasher or do you have to wash the (dish) _____ yourself?

10. (teenager) _____ often dream of becoming (celebrity) _____ because they think that they must lead such glamourous (life) _____.

Nomen/*nouns*

Nomen, die nur im Singular stehen

Das ist wichtig!

Nomen wie *homework, information, news, furniture, proof, advice* und *hair* sind im Englischen unzählbar – sie haben **keine Pluralform**:

Diese Informationen sind vertraulich.
This information **is** confidential.

!**Merke**

Bei Nomen, die nur im Singular gebraucht werden, stehen die dazugehörigen **Verben** und **Pronomen auch** im **Singular**.

Übung 2

Translate the words in brackets ().

1. Teenagers often read teen magazines for (*Ratschläge*)

   _advice_____ on fashion and style.

2. Amy has brown eyes and beautiful long dark (*Haare*) _____.

3. Sophie thinks she knows who stole her purse, but she has no (*Beweise*)

   _____.

4. Have you seen these brochures? They have some very useful (*Informationen*) _____ on how to help the environment.

5. (*Die Hausaufgaben waren*) _____

   too difficult. None of the children could do (*sie*) _____.

6. I'm afraid (*die Nachrichten sind*) _____ not good.

   Are you sure that you want to hear (*sie*) _____?

7. I didn't like their new (*Möbel*) _____. (*Sie waren*)

   _____ very uncomfortable.

Nomen, die nur im Plural stehen

Das ist wichtig!

Folgende Nomen werden im Englischen **nur im Plural** gebraucht: *scissors, trousers, pants, pyjamas, shorts, glasses, police, clothes, stairs*:

Diese Hose ist zu kurz.
These trousers **are** too short.

> **! Merke**
>
> Bei Nomen, die nur im Plural gebraucht werden, stehen die dazugehörigen **Verben** und **Pronomen auch** im **Plural**.

Übung 3

Translate the words in brackets ().

1. Amy wanted to wear her new (*Hose*) _____ to the party, but she couldn't find (*sie*) _____. (*Sie war*) _____ under her bed.

2. Do you know where (*meine Brille ist*) _____? – Yes, I saw (*sie*) _____ on the kitchen table a moment ago.

3. (*Die Treppe war*) _____ very dirty. (*Sie*) _____ hadn't been cleaned for a long time.

4. Somebody has called the police. (*Sie kommt*) _____. (*Sie wird*) _____ be here in a minute.

5. (*Diese Schere ist*) _____ no good. (*Sie ist nicht*) _____ sharp enough.

6. Kate hadn't put her washing into the basket. (*Ihre schmutzige Kleidung lag*) _____ on her bedroom floor.

7. (*Deine neue Hose gefällt mir. Sie sieht gut aus!*) I like _____ good.

Nomen/*nouns*

some/a piece of/a pair of

Das ist wichtig!

Vor **unzählbaren Nomen** wie *information, news, furniture* und *advice* wird statt *a/an* **some** oder *a piece of* verwendet:

Tom hat mir einen guten Rat gegeben.
Tom gave me **some** good advice.
Tom gave me **a** good **piece of** advice.

Ähnlich ist es bei den **Paarwörtern** wie *scissors, glasses* oder *trousers*. Für „ein (-e, -en)" verwendest du *some* oder *a pair of*:

Gestern habe ich mir eine neue Hose gekauft.
I bought **some** new trousers yesterday.
I bought **a** new **pair of** trousers yesterday.

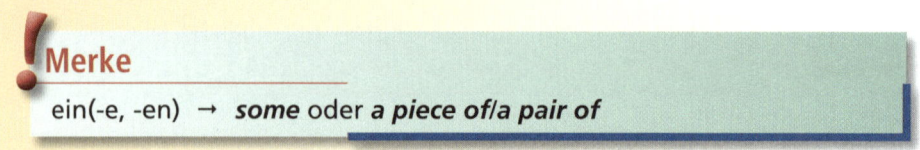

> **! Merke**
>
> ein(-e, -en) → *some* oder *a piece of/a pair of*

Und wenn Tom dir **zwei (drei, …)** gute Ratschläge gegeben hat oder du dir **zwei (drei, …)** neue Hosen gekauft hast, dann sagst du:

Tom gave me **two (three, …)** good **pieces of** advice.
I bought **two (three, …)** new **pairs of** trousers yesterday.

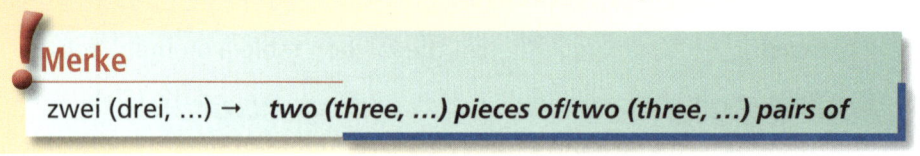

> **! Merke**
>
> zwei (drei, …) → *two (three, …) pieces of/two (three, …) pairs of*

Übung 4

Finish the sentences.

1. Ich gebe dir einen guten Rat.
   I'll give you _some good advice._
   (or) I'll give you _a good piece of advice._

2. Ich suche eine Schere.
   I'm looking for _____.
   (or) I'm looking for _____.
   Da sind zwei Scheren in der Schublade.
   There are _____ in the drawer.

3 Ich brauche einen neuen Schlafanzug.

   I need _____.

   (or) I need _____.

4 Ich habe eine interessante Neuigkeit für dich.

   I have _____ for you.

   (or) I have _____ for you.

Das Stützwort *one/ones*

Das ist wichtig!

Schau dir dieses Beispiel an:

Da waren drei Goldfische im Teich – zwei große und ein kleiner.
There were three goldfish in the pond – two big **ones** and one little **one**.

> **! Merke**
> 1 Mit *one* oder *ones* **vermeidest** du die **Wiederholung** eines vorangegangenen Nomens.
> 2 *one* oder *ones* steht **oft nach einem Adjektiv**.

Übung 5

Finish these sentences.

1 The chairs were all broken, so we had to buy (*neue*)

   _____.

2 The train had left, so we had to wait for (*den nächsten*)

   _____.

3 Which T-shirt do you like better? (*Das rote oder das gelbe*)

   _____?

4 Those trousers don't look very nice. Why don't you buy (*eine neue*)

   _____?

Nomen/*nouns*

Der Genitiv

Das ist wichtig!

Der **Genitiv (Wessen-Fall)** wird mit *'s, s'* oder *of* gebildet. Der *s*-**Genitiv** wird bei **Personen, Tieren** und bei **Zeit- und Ortsangaben** verwendet, der *of*-**Genitiv** bei **Sachen**.

Verwende **Apostroph + s** (= *'s*)
bei **Nomen** im **Singular** und bei **Nomen** im **Plural**, die **nicht auf -s enden**,
bei **Ortsangaben** (Staaten, Städte und Institutionen),
bei **Zeitangaben**:

das Fahrrad des Kindes	→	the child's bike
die Fahrräder der Kinder	→	the children's bikes
die besten Strände Großbritanniens	→	Britain's best beaches
beim Zahnarzt	→	at the dentist's
die Welt von morgen	→	tomorrow's world

Verwende **s + Apostroph** (= *s'*) bei **Nomen** im **Plural**, die **auf -s enden**:

die Schlafzimmer der Mädchen	→	the girls' bedrooms
das Haus der Nachbarn	→	the neighbours' house

Verwende *of* bei **Sachen** oder nach *hundreds/thousands*:

die Folgen der Erderwärmung	→	the consequences **of** global warming
der erste Buchstabe des Alphabets	→	the first letter **of** the alphabet
Hunderte von Menschen	→	hundreds **of** people

!**Merke**

1 *s*-**Genitiv** bei **Personen, Tieren** und **Orts- und Zeitangaben**.
2 *of*-**Genitiv** bei **Sachen**.

Übung 6

Translate the words in brackets ().

1 Uncle Jim is (*der Bruder meines Vaters*)

_____.

2 (*Der Gewinner des Wettbewerbs*) _____

_____ will receive 100,000 euros.

3 Ben isn't here at the moment. He's (*beim Arzt*)

_____.

Der Genitiv

4 Have you read (*die Zeitung von heute*)
   _____?

5 All the actors performed well but (*der Star der Show*)
   _____ was an eleven-year-old girl.

6 The Native Americans had already been living in the country for
   (*Tausende von Jahren*) _____
   before the white man came.

7 There were (*Hunderte von Menschen*)
   _____ on the beach.

8 You will find (*eine Liste von den unregelmäßigen Verben auf der letzten Seite deines Englischbuches*) _____
   _____.

9 Do you know (*die Namen von den Söhnen von Charles*)
   _____?

10 The Statue of Liberty is (*eine der beliebtesten Touristenattraktionen New Yorks*)
   _____

	Das kann ich hier üben!	**Das kann ich jetzt!**	☺	😐	☹
	Ich beherrsche die Bildung von regelmäßigen und unregelmäßigen Pluralformen.		☐	☐	☐
	Ich kenne mich mit Nomen aus, die im Englischen nur im Singular stehen.		☐	☐	☐
	Ich kenne mich mit Nomen aus, die im Englischen nur im Plural stehen.		☐	☐	☐
	Ich beherrsche die Verwendung von *some*/*a piece of*/*a pair of* bei unzählbaren Nomen.		☐	☐	☐
	Mir ist klar, wann und wie ich das Stützwort *one*/*ones* verwende.		☐	☐	☐
	Mit dem Genitiv kenne ich mich aus.		☐	☐	☐

Der bestimmte und der unbestimmte Artikel

Das kann ich hier üben! Das kann ich jetzt!

- ☐ Konkrete und abstrakte Begriffe mit und ohne bestimmten Artikel
- ☐ Mahlzeiten, Nahrungsmittel und Stoffe mit und ohne bestimmten Artikel
- ☐ Den bestimmten Artikel bei Gebirgen, Gewässern und Ländernamen
- ☐ Den bestimmten Artikel bei Straßen, Parks und Sehenswürdigkeiten
- ☐ Verkehrsmittel und Institutionen mit und ohne bestimmten Artikel
- ☐ *most*, *most of the*, *the most*
- ☐ Den unbestimmten Artikel (*a/an*)
- ☐ Den unbestimmten Artikel nach *half*, *quite* und *such*

Konkrete und abstrakte Begriffe mit und ohne bestimmten Artikel

Das ist wichtig!

Nomen können **konkret** oder **abstrakt** sein: *concrete nouns* sind **Objekte**, die du **sehen und anfassen** kannst, wie z. B. „das Gebäude" oder „der Stuhl", **einschließlich Menschen und Tiere**. Das Gegenteil davon sind *abstract nouns* – das sind **Ideen oder Gefühle**, die du **weder sehen noch anfassen** kannst, wie z. B. „das Leben", „das Glück", „die Liebe", „die Musik" usw.
Schau dir diese Beispiele an:

ohne Artikel	mit bestimmtem Artikel
Children can be noisy.	**The** children **who live next door** can be very noisy.
Life can be hard.	**The** life **of a pop star** can be hard.

❗ Merke

1. **Begriffe** (*concrete nouns* und *abstract nouns*), die im allgemeinen Sinne gebraucht werden, stehen **ohne *the***.
2. **Begriffe** (*concrete nouns* und *abstract nouns*), die **näher bestimmt** werden, **oft** durch einen **Relativsatz** oder ein *of* + **Nomen**, stehen **mit *the***.

Konkrete und abstrakte Begriffe mit und ohne bestimmten Artikel

Übung 1

Put in the definite article where necessary.

1. _____ Life/life of a pop star isn't always glamourous.

2. _____ History/history is not Dan's favourite subject. The only history he is interested in is _____ history of rock music.

3. _____ Immigrants/immigrants who arrived in America between 1820 and 1920 came mainly from Europe.

4. _____ Immigrants/immigrants are people who have left their home countries and now live in a different country.

5. Do you like _____ Indian food? _____ Curries/curries they serve at the new Indian restaurant are delicious.

6. Mrs Davis enjoys working with _____ children. _____ Children/children she works with are all very well-behaved.

Übung 2

Translation practice.

1. Das Leben in den Reservaten ist sehr schwer.

2. Die *Native Americans*, die dort leben, haben oft keine Arbeit.

3. Der Tourismus ist für sie eine wichtige Industrie.

4. Manche Leute meinen, dass Touristenattraktionen wie der *Grand Canyon Skywalk* die natürliche Landschaft zerstören (*to destroy*) werden.

Der bestimmte und der unbestimmte Artikel

Mahlzeiten, Nahrungsmittel und Stoffe mit und ohne bestimmten Artikel

Das ist wichtig!

Schau dir diese Beispiele an:	
ohne Artikel	**mit bestimmtem Artikel**
After lunch we played a game.	**The** lunch **Kate cooked for us** was delicious.
We can't live without water.	**The** water **you buy in bottles** isn't expensive.

! Merke

Verwende *the* vor Mahlzeiten, Nahrungsmitteln oder Stoffen **nur, wenn** sie (meist durch einen Relativsatz) **näher bestimmt** werden.

Übung 3

Put in the definite article where necessary.

1 All children should drink _____ milk.

2 _____ Milk/milk that is in the fridge is already sour.

3 For _____ breakfast Tom had a bowl of cornflakes and two pieces of toast.

4 _____ Fish/fish we buy from the market is always very fresh.

5 _____ Food/food at the restaurant was badly cooked and it was cold.

Übung 4

Translation practice.

1 Zum Frühstück aß ich eine Scheibe Toast.

   _____.

2 Ich rufe dich nach dem Mittagessen an.

   _____.

3 Das Mittagessen, das Anna für uns gekocht hat, war lecker.

   _____
   _____.

Der bestimmte Artikel bei Gebirgen, Gewässern und Ländernamen

Das ist wichtig!

Schau dir diese Beispiele an:	
ohne Artikel	**mit bestimmtem Artikel**
Berge: *Mount Everest, Mount McKinley*	**Gebirge:** *the Alps*, *the Rocky Mountains*
Seen: *Lake Constance, Loch Ness*	**Meere:** *the Atlantic*, *the Pacific*
Ländernamen im Singular: *England, France, Switzerland*	**Ländernamen im Plural:** *the USA*, *the UK*, *the Netherlands*
	Flüsse: *the Rhine*, *the Colorado River*

Übung 5

Put in the definite article where necessary.

1 _____ Lake/lake Constance is the English name for the *Bodensee*.

2 _____ Colorado River has been winding its way through the Grand Canyon for millions of years.

3 _____ Mount/mount McKinley is the highest mountain in _____ USA.

4 Where is the best snow for skiing? In _____ Alps or in _____ Rocky Mountains?

5 Dutch is the language that people speak in _____ Netherlands.

Übung 6

Translation practice.

1 Der *Mount Everest* ist der höchste Berg der Welt.

2 Weißt du, wie lang der *Colorado River* ist?

3 Lars war schon zweimal in England, aber er war noch nie in den USA.

Der bestimmte Artikel bei Straßen, Parks und Sehenswürdigkeiten

Das ist wichtig!

Schau dir diese Beispiele an:	
ohne Artikel	**mit bestimmtem Artikel**
Straßen: *Fifth Avenue, 65th Street, Broadway* **Parks:** *Central Park*	
Eigennamen: *downtown, Manhattan, Ground Zero, Ellis Island, Liberty Island, Chinatown*	**Eigennamen: the** *Big Apple,* **the** *Statue of Liberty,* **the** *Empire State Building,* **the** *Brooklyn Bridge*

Übung 7

How much do you know about New York?

1. You'll find a lot of theatres here. _____
2. The place where the early immigrants arrived. _____
3. It's another name for New York. _____
4. It's the cultural center of New York City. _____
5. If you like Chinese food, this is the place to go. _____
6. It's the American word for the "city centre". _____
7. It was a present from the French. _____
8. The place where the World Trade Center once stood. _____
9. A famous shopping street in Manhattan. _____
10. A famous skyscraper and tourist attraction. _____
11. A place where you can relax. _____
12. A famous bridge over the East River. _____

Verkehrsmittel und Institutionen mit und ohne bestimmten Artikel

Das ist wichtig!

Schau dir diese Beispiele an:	
ohne Artikel	**mit bestimmtem Artikel**
Dad usually goes to work by train.	He normally catches **the 7.20** train.
The children are at school all day.	**The** school **they go to** is close by.

> **! Merke**
>
> Verwende *the* vor Verkehrsmitteln und Institutionen wie *school, church, prison* oder *hospital* **nur, wenn** sie **näher bestimmt** werden.

Übung 8

Put in the definite article where necessary.

1. Amy is in _____ hospital. She's in _____ hospital in King's Road.
2. Ben's parents go to _____ church every Sunday. _____ Church/church they go to is 800 years old.
3. Jack is in _____ prison. His father can't visit him because _____ prison he is in is too far away.
4. Amy usually goes to school by _____ bike or by _____ train, but sometimes her mother takes her in _____ car.

Übung 9

Translation practice.

1. Kates Bruder ist im Krankenhaus.

2. Wir fahren zum Flughafen mit dem Zug.

3. Die Schule, die Amy besucht, hat über 800 Schüler.

Der bestimmte und der unbestimmte Artikel

most, most of the, the most
Das ist wichtig!

Schau dir diese Beispiele an:	
most (= fast alle Leute ohne Einschränkung)	
***Most** people like ice-cream.*	Die meisten Leute mögen Eis.
most of the (= fast alle aus einer beschränkten Zahl)	
***Most of the** people I know like ice-cream.*	Die meisten Leute, die ich kenne, mögen Eis.
the most + adjective (= 2. Steigerungsform)	
***the most** boring film*	der langweiligste Film
***the most** important man*	der wichtigste Mann

Übung 10

Complete these sentences with 'most', 'most of the' or 'the most'.

1 Today _____ children have TVs in their bedroom.

2 _____ children in Tom's class have TVs in their bedroom.

3 I didn't know everybody at the party but I knew _____ people.

4 Tom has already read _____ Harry Potter books.

5 She had _____ beautiful eyes I had ever seen, one was blue and two were green.

Übung 11

Translation practice.

1 Die meisten Kinder schwimmen gern.

_____

2 Die meisten Kinder unserer Klasse wohnen in der Nähe von der Schule.

_____

_____

3 Die meisten Arbeitsplätze in der Stadt sind im Tourismus.

_____

Der unbestimmte Artikel (a/an)

Das ist wichtig!

Der unbestimmte Artikel (a/an) steht im Englischen **vor**:

Berufsbezeichnungen	Mr Black ist Schauspieler. Mr Black is **an** actor.	Seine Frau ist Pilotin. His wife is **a** pilot.
Maßeinheiten (= pro/je)	2 Euro das Pfund 2 euros **a** pound	4 Euro das Kilo 4 euros **a** kilogram
Zeitangaben (= pro/je)	einmal am Tag once **a** day	zweimal die Woche twice **a** week
100 und **1000**	100/1000 **a** 100/**a** 1000	hundert/tausend **a** hundred/**a** thousand

Übung 12

Complete the sentences below with words from the box. Remember to add a/an.

~~engineer~~ – hundred – teacher – day – year – thousand – week – kilo

1 Kate's father is _an engineer_ and her mother is _____.

2 The school is quite large. It has almost _____ students.

3 If you say that a restaurant is open 24/7, you mean that it is open 24 hours _____, seven days _____.

4 The school orchestra gives a concert twice _____, one is in December and the other is in June.

5 How many pence are there in a pound? – _____.

6 How much do the tomatoes cost? – Two pounds _____.

Übung 13

Translation practice.

1 Wie viel Taschengeld kriegst du im Monat? – 50 Euro.

2 Wie lange wartest du schon? – Seit einer halben Stunde!

3 Tom: „Wie viel kostet das Hotel?"

Der bestimmte und der unbestimmte Artikel

David: „Hundert Dollar pro Nacht."

Tom: „Hundert Dollar? Das ist zu viel."

Der unbestimmte Artikel nach *half, quite* und *such*
Das ist wichtig!

Der unbestimmte Artikel (*a/an*) steht im Englischen **nach**:		
half	Ich rufe dich in einer halben Stunde an.	I'll call you in **half an** hour.
	Wir brauchen ein halbes Pfund Mehl.	We need **half a** pound of flour.
quite	Es war eine ziemlich lustige Geschichte.	It was **quite a** funny story.
such	Wir hatten so einen schönen Urlaub.	We had **such a** good holiday.

Übung 14

Complete the sentences below using words from the box. Remember to add a/an.

> quite/amusing ending – half/pound – such/idiot – half/mile – ~~such/beautiful day~~ – half/hour – quite/long time – such/noise – such/mess

1. Why don't we go to the beach? It's such a beautiful day.
2. Do we need anything from the shops? – Yes, a loaf of bread and _____ of butter.
3. When does the film start? – In about _____.
4. I don't like Ben. I think he's _____.
5. It took _____ but in the end we managed to install the new software.
6. Please don't make _____, I'm trying to concentrate.
7. Is it far from here to the station? – No, not really. It's only about _____.
8. Did you enjoy the film? – Yes, it had _____.
9. Jack, your room is in _____. Please tidy it now.

Der unbestimmte Artikel nach *half*, *quite* und *such*

Übung 15

Translation practice.

1. Ich gehe einkaufen. Brauchst du etwas? – Ja, ein halbes Pfund Butter.

2. Mach nicht so einen Krach!

3. Sophie hat mir gestern einen ganz lustigen Witz erzählt.

Das kann ich hier üben!	**Das kann ich jetzt!**	☺	😐	☹
Ich weiß, was *concrete nouns* und *abstract nouns* sind und wann sie mit bzw. ohne bestimmten Artikel stehen.		❏	❏	❏
Mir ist geläufig, wann der bestimmte Artikel bei Mahlzeiten, Nahrungsmitteln und Stoffen steht.		❏	❏	❏
Ich weiß, wann der bestimmte Artikel bei Gebirgen, Gewässern und Ländernamen verwendet wird.		❏	❏	❏
Ich weiß Bescheid über den bestimmten Artikel bei Straßen, Parks und Sehenswürdigkeiten.		❏	❏	❏
Mir ist geläufig, wann der bestimmte Artikel bei Verkehrsmitteln und Institution gesetzt werden muss.		❏	❏	❏
Die Verwendung von *the* im Zusammenhang mit *most* habe ich begriffen.		❏	❏	❏
Mir ist klar, vor welchen Begriffen der unbestimmte Artikel steht.		❏	❏	❏
Ich kann den unbestimmten Artikel nach *half*, *quite* und *such* sicher verwenden.		❏	❏	❏

Notwendige und nicht notwendige Relativsätze

Das kann ich hier üben! **Das kann ich jetzt!**

- ❏ Notwendige Relativsätze und Relativpronomen
- ❏ Bildung und Verwendung von *contact clauses*
- ❏ *contact clauses* mit Präpositionen
- ❏ Nicht notwendige Relativsätze
- ❏ Die Bedeutung von Kommas in Relativsätzen

Notwendige Relativsätze

Das ist wichtig!

Ein notwendiger Relativsatz bestimmt das **Bezugswort** im Hauptsatz näher. Im Deutschen wird er mit einem **Relativpronomen** („der", „die", „das", „den", „dessen", „deren" oder „wo") eingeleitet:

*Tim is **the boy who** (or **that**) never does his homework.* (… der Junge, der …)
***The bears which** (or **that**) live in Yellowstone Park are* (… die Bären, die …)
*Amy is **the girl whose** mother is American.* (… das Mädchen, dessen Mutter …)
*This is **the cupboard where** we keep our books.* (… der Schrank, wo …)
*Grammar is **something that** you have to learn.* (… etwas, das …)

> **! Merke**
>
> 1. Im Englischen heißen die Relativpronomen *who*, *which*, *that*, *whose* oder *where*.
> 2. *who* (oder *that*) benutzt du für **Personen**.
> 3. *which* (oder *that*) benutzt du für **Sachen und Tiere**.
> 4. *whose* wird für **Sachen und Personen** verwendet.
> 5. Nach *something, everything, all* und *nothing* steht *that* (nicht *which*)!
> 6. Zwischen Hauptsatz und Relativsatz steht **kein Komma**.

Übung 1

Complete these sentences with who, which, that, whose oder where.

1. Blogging is a leisure pursuit _____ is becoming more and more popular.

2 Weblogs, or blogs for short, are diaries _____ people write online.
3 For those _____ enjoy sharing their feelings with the world, the Internet is a great place to be.
4 The problem is that the Internet is also a place _____ many people feel anonymous.
5 Not everything _____ people write online is acceptable.
6 Sometimes the things _____ they blog about can be very hurtful to others.
7 That is why some people's websites _____ blogs are too personal are often shut down, and rightly so.

Was ist ein *contact clause*?

Das ist wichtig!

Als *contact clause* wird ein **Relativsatz (*relative clause*) ohne Relativpronomen** bezeichnet:

relative clause: The money **that we collected** was for charity.
contact clause: The money **we collected** was for charity.

> **Merke**
> 1 Wenn der Relativsatz ein **eigenes Subjekt** hat (hier *we*), kann man das **einleitende Relativpronomen** (*who*, *that* oder *which*) einfach **weglassen**.
> 2 Ein **Relativpronomen** mit **anschließendem Verb** darfst du **nie weglassen**.
> 3 Das Relativpronomen *whose* darfst du **nie weglassen**.

Übung 2

In which of these sentences can you leave out the relative pronoun? If you can leave it out, draw a line through it.

1 The book ~~that~~ I'm reading at the moment is really sad.
2 It's about a young girl whose parents have died.
3 She's a brave girl who isn't easily frightened.
4 The people who she lives with are not always kind to her.
5 Nothing that she does is ever good enough for them.
6 Her bedroom is a small room which she has to share with three other children.

contact clauses mit Präpositionen

Das ist wichtig!

Beim *contact clause* mit Präposition wird das Relativpronomen weggelassen und die **Präposition ans Ende des Relativsatzes** gesetzt:

relative clause: The hotel **at which we stayed** was close to the beach.
relative clause: The hotel **which we stayed at** was close to the beach.
contact clause: The hotel **we stayed at** was close to the beach.

Übung 3

Look at the example. Then change the sentences the same way.

1   We stayed at a camp-site which was very modern.

    The camp-site we stayed at was very modern.

2   I slept in a bed which was very comfortable.

    The

3   I spoke to some park rangers who were all very friendly.

4   We went on some excursions which were fantastic fun.

5   I took photos of some trees which were about four thousand years old.

6   I made friends with some people who are going to visit me next summer.

Notwendige und nicht notwendige Relativsätze verglichen

Das ist wichtig!

Ein **notwendiger Relativsatz bestimmt** das **Bezugswort im Hauptsatz** näher:
The boy (who) Kate met on holiday is a drummer in a band.
Ohne den Relativsatz *who Kate met on holiday* würden wir nicht wissen, von welchem Jungen die Rede ist.

Beim **nicht notwendigen Relativsatz** ist das **Bezugswort** im Hauptsatz bereits **klar definiert** – oft durch einen Eigennamen – und braucht daher keine weitere Erklärung:
Tom, who Kate met on holiday, is a drummer in a band.
Hier geht es eindeutig um Tom. Der Relativsatz *who Kate met on holiday* stellt daher nur eine **Zusatzinformation** dar.

> **! Merke**
>
> Ist das Bezugswort im Hauptsatz bereits bestimmt,
> 1. musst du den **Relativsatz in Kommas setzen** und
> 2. das **Relativpronomen einsetzen**.
> 3. **Mögliche Relativpronomen** sind *who, which, whose* oder *where*, aber **niemals** *that*.

Übung 4

Decide which of these relative clauses are defining and which are non-defining. Add commas where necessary.

1. The team who beat us in the semi-finals went on to win the tournament.
2. Gordon High who beat us in the semi-finals went on to win the tournament.
3. The tournament was held at the new stadium which was built last year.
4. Each year it is an event which is very popular.
5. Ben who scored the winning goal is only 15 years old.
6. The boy who scored the winning goal is only 15 years old.
7. Ben's father who was a famous footballer himself was at the match to support him.
8. The man in the stands who kept jumping up and down was Ben's father.
9. The woman who was sitting next to him was his mother.
10. Ben whose mother was a tennis star is also an excellent tennis player.

Notwendige und nicht notwendige Relativsätze

Die Bedeutung von Kommas in Relativsätzen

Das ist wichtig!

Schau dir diese Beispiele an:

1. The girls who wanted to play tennis were disappointed when it rained.
   → **Nur** die Mädchen, die Tennis spielen wollten, waren enttäuscht.
2. The girls, who wanted to play tennis, were disappointed when it rained.
   → **Alle** Mädchen wollten Tennis spielen, und sie waren **alle** enttäuscht.

!**Merke**

1. **Ohne Kommas** wird das **Bezugswort näher bestimmt**, um eine Verwechselung mit anderen zu vermeiden.
2. **Mit Kommas** ist das **Bezugswort bereits klar definiert**. Es kann keine Verwechselung geben.

Übung 5

Explain the meaning of the sentences.

1a The teacher told the students, who hadn't finished the exercise, to do it for homework.

1b The teacher told the students who hadn't finished the exercise to do it for homework.

2a Tom's sister who emigrated to the USA lives in Los Angeles.

2b Tom's sister, who emigrated to the USA, lives in Los Angeles.

Die Bedeutung von Kommas in Relativsätzen

3a The clothes which were on the floor were all dirty.

_____

_____

3b The clothes, which were on the floor, were all dirty.

_____

_____

Übung 6

Fill in the relative pronouns. If you can leave them out, draw a line through them. Add commas where necessary.

The Native Americans

1 The first people to arrive in America came from Asia about 20,000 years ago. They were people__ _____ moved from place to place in search of food.

2 They crossed the Bering Sound[1]__ _____ at that time formed a land bridge between the two continents of Asia and America.

3 The European settlers__ _____ began arriving in the 1600s__ called these people Indians because the first people__ _____ had sailed from Europe to America__ thought that they had arrived in India.

4 At first, the Indians__ _____ were mostly peaceful people__ welcomed the new settlers and even helped them to survive.

5 But conflicts between them arose soon when the white man began to take land for themselves__ _____ the Indians believed belonged to everyone.

6 The land was very important for the Indians__ _____ lives were close to nature__ but the Europeans could not understand this.

---

[1] *Bering Sound* = Beringstraße

Notwendige und nicht notwendige Relativsätze

7 They believed that land__ _____ hadn't been fenced² in__ didn't belong to anyone.

8 To solve the problem, the American government decided to move all the Indian tribes__ _____ were living in the Southwest__ to the west of the Mississippi river__ _____ they would be given new land. The journey was long and hard and many of the Cherokee Indians died on the way. Those__ _____ survived__ called it "The Trail of Tears".

9 After 1848, more and more white Americans__ _____ were hoping to find gold in California__ crossed the Mississippi into Indian territory.

10 Wars broke out and thousands of Indians were killed. By 1900 those__ _____ were left__ were forced to live on reservations.

11 As one Indian chief put it: "The white man made many promises to the Indians, but there was only one promise__ _____ he kept: the one to take our land."

12 Life on the reservations__ _____ there were few jobs__ was hard and many of the Indians became alcoholics or died of white man's diseases.

13 Today the Indians__ _____ are now known as Native Americans__ no longer have to live on reservations. They can live in any city__ _____ they wish to.

14 There are many of them__ _____ have managed to lead successful lives. Some have become teachers, doctors or lawyers, and there are others__ _____ have even become the bosses of billion-dollar businesses.

---

2 *fenced in* = eingezäunt

Die Bedeutung von Kommas in Relativsätzen

Übung 7

Fill in the relative pronouns. If you can leave them out, draw a line through them. Add commas where necessary.

The Skywalk

1 The Skywalk__ _____ was opened in March 2007__ is the Grand Canyon's latest attraction.

2 The views__ _____ you get from the horseshoe-shaped glass observation platform of the Canyon 4,000 feet below__ are awesome.

3 With this project the Hualapai Indians__ _____ own the site__ are hoping to tackle[3] the problems of high unemployment[4] on their reservation.

4 They feel that this is an investment which will bring them the money__ _____ they desperately need.

5 But there are some people__ _____ are not so happy about this new tourist attraction.

6 They are afraid that the highway__ _____ the tribe plans to build in order to attract more visitors__ will destroy the natural beauty of the land.

---
3 *to tackle* = angehen
4 *unemployment* = Arbeitslosigkeit

Notwendige und nicht notwendige Relativsätze

Übung 8

Fill in the relative pronouns. If you can leave them out, draw a line through them. Add commas where necessary.

The Mayflower Compact

1 In 1620 the Mayflower set sail from Plymouth in Britain for Virginia – a colony __ _____ had been founded in the New World by British settlers in 1607.

2 On board were 35 Puritans – a religious group __ _____ had not been allowed to practise their religion freely in Britain __ – as well as a number of other passengers __ _____ wanted to leave Britain for different reasons.

3 The voyage __ _____ took 66 days __ was long and hard.

4 When they finally reached the New World, they didn't land in Virginia, but further north at a place __ _____ few Europeans had been before.

5 They called their new home Plymouth after the port __ _____ they had sailed from in Britain.

6 Before landing, the Puritans wrote down a set of rules __ _____ everybody had to agree to follow.

7 This Agreement __ _____ later became known as The Mayflower Compact __ was the beginning of democracy in America.

Übung 9

Join these two sentences using relative clauses. Decide where you need commas.

1 Kate was dancing with William. She looked very happy.

_____

_____

2 Ben threw the ball to Jack. He then threw it to me.

_____

_____

3 Jack lives with his mother. His parents split up before he was born.

_____

_____

Die Bedeutung von Kommas in Relativsätzen

4   I was travelling on a bus. It was almost empty.

5   I know a good restaurant. We can have lunch there.

6   "The Mayflower" serves very good food. We had lunch there yesterday.

7   A German family live in that house. Do you know them?

8   You were looking for your sunglasses. Did you find them?

Das kann ich hier üben!	**Das kann ich jetzt!**	😊	😐	☹
Ich weiß, was ein notwendiger Relativsatz ist.		☐	☐	☐
Ich kenne die Relativpronomen *who, which, that, whose* und *where* und weiß, wie sie benutzt werden.		☐	☐	☐
Ich weiß, was *contact clauses* sind und wie man sie verwendet.		☐	☐	☐
Ich kann *contact clauses* mit Präpositionen bilden.		☐	☐	☐
Ich weiß, wie ein nicht notwendiger Relativsatz gebildet wird und wie er sich von einem notwendigen Relativsatz unterscheidet.		☐	☐	☐
Mir ist klar, welche Bedeutung die Kommas bei Relativsätzen haben.		☐	☐	☐

Adjektive und Adverbien

Das kann ich hier üben! **Das kann ich jetzt!**

- ❏ Den Unterschied zwischen Adjektiven und Adverbien
- ❏ Das Adjektiv nach Zustandsverben
- ❏ Partizipien als Adjektive
- ❏ Die Stellung der Adverbien der Häufigkeit, der Adverbien der Art und Weise und der Adverbialen des Ortes und der Zeit

Was ist ein Adjektiv und was ein Adverb?

Das ist wichtig!

Schau dir diese Beispiele an:
1 Jack *is a* **polite** *boy.* → Adjektiv
2 Jack *always* **speaks politely**. → Adverb

!**Merke**

1 Das **Adjektiv** beschreibt, **wie** man **ist**.
2 Das **Adverb** beschreibt, **wie** man etwas **tut**.

Übung 1

Complete the sentences with a word from the box. Decide if you need an adjective or an adverb.

regular – expensive – popular – free – thrilling – right – safe

1 Horse riding is a _____ sport in the UK.
2 Over 4 million people go riding _____.
3 It can be a _____ experience, but only if you do it _____.
4 You should wear a riding hat, boots and clothing that lets you move _____.
5 Riding is an _____ hobby, so before you buy all the equipment, you should make sure that it is the _____ one for you.

Das Adjektiv nach Zustandsverben

Das ist wichtig!

Schau dir diese Beispiele an:

1 Kate **looks unhappy**. → Adjektiv
2 The cholcolate cake **tastes delicious**. → Adjektiv

> **! Merke**
>
> Hinter **Verben**, die einen **Zustand** oder eine **Sinneswahrnehmung** ausdrücken, wie *to feel, to look* (aussehen), *to smell, to sound, to taste, to become/to get* (werden), *to seem/to appear* (scheinen), *to remain/to keep/to stay* (bleiben) **steht** auch das **Adjektiv**.

Übung 2

Complete the sentences with a word from the box. Decide if you need an adjective or an adverb.

powerful – natural – nervous – scared – calm – relaxed – angry

1 Horses are _____ animals, so it is quite _____ for you to feel a little _____ at first.

2 But remember that a horse can sense immediately if its rider is _____.

3 So you must show him who is in control. But never get _____. Just try to stay as _____ and _____ as you can.

Adjektive und Adverbien

Partizipien als Adjektive

Das ist wichtig!

Das *present participle* (Verb + -*ing*) und das *past participle* (3. Form des Verbs) können **als Adjektiv** vor einem Nomen stehen:

ein langweiliger Film   ein gelangweiltes Publikum
a **boring** film   a **bored** audience

Übung 3

Put in the right word.

handpainted – amusing – growing – shocked – strange-looking – tree-lined – unexpected

1 Exeter is a town with a _____ population.

2 Do you know who that rather _____ man is?

3 The _____ vases were magnificent.

4 Yesterday I heard a very _____ story.

5 The house was at the end of a beautiful _____ avenue.

6 The whole world was _____ by Princess Diana's sudden and _____ death in 1997.

Übung 4

Fill in the missing adjectives. Use the present or past participle of one of the following verbs.

to frighten – to fly – to break – to surprise – to disappoint – to excite – to mix – to wait – to steal – ~~to interest~~

1 I met Jo yesterday. We had a very _interesting_ chat.

2 Sophie cut her foot on some _____ glass.

150

Partizipien als Adjektive

3   Nobody was killed in the explosion but a lot of people were injured by _____ glass.

4   The film had a _____ ending.

5   Yesterday police raided a factory in Old Road and recovered a number of _____ cars.

6   The _____ girl hid under the bed.

7   Toby is a talented actor with an _____ future ahead of him.

8   I don't know if I want to see the film. It has been given very _____ reviews.

9   Kate was most _____ when she wasn't offered the job as a model.

10 The bank robber rushed out of the bank and jumped into a _____ car.

Übung 5

Shorten the following sentences using a present participle + noun clause or a past participle + noun clause.

1   Allsops is a company which is growing very fast.

    Allsops is a fast growing company.

2   Tom asked a question that we found very interesting.

    _____

3   The teacher advised the pupils not to read books that had been written badly.

    _____

4   Jack told me a story which I found amusing.

    _____

Adjektive und Adverbien

Die Stellung von Adverbien – Adverbien der Häufigkeit

Das ist wichtig!

Schau dir diese Beispiele an:

1 Tim **usually walks** to school.
2 He **doesn't always get** to school on time.
3 He **is often** late.

!**Merke**

Adverbien der Häufigkeit wie *always, never, often, usually, normally, sometimes, hardly ever, rarely* und *seldom* stehen **meist vor dem Hauptverb** und **immer hinter** einer Form von *to be*.

Übung 6

Where do these words belong?

1 The bus _____ runs _____ on time. (usually)

2 _____ Read/read _____ the instructions before you do the exercise. (always)

3 Ben _____ isn't _____ at home in the evenings. (often)

4 Emily _____ listens _____ in class. (never)

5 Jane _____ doesn't _____ do her homework. (always)

6 We _____ visit _____ our grandparents at the weekends. (sometimes)

7 It _____ doesn't _____ snow in the winter. (often)

8 Tim and Amy _____ aren't _____ late for school. (usually)

9 We _____ go _____ to bed before 10 pm. (hardly ever)

10 Ben _____ has _____ had to work hard. (always)

Die Stellung von Adverbien – Adverbien der Art und Weise

Das ist wichtig!

Schau dir diese Beispiele an:

1 The children always <u>listen</u> **carefully** in class.
2 The children <u>read</u> the instructions **carefully**.
3 The children **carefully** <u>read</u> all the instructions on the paper.

> **! Merke**
>
> Adverbien der Art und Weise wie *carefully, quickly, slowly, loudly, quietly, well, badly* usw. stehen
> 1 **hinter** dem **Verb**,
> 2 **hinter Verb + Objekt**,
> 3 **vor** dem **Verb**, wenn das **Objekt lang** ist.

Übung 7

Where do these words belong?

1 The children laughed ⬇. (loudly)

2 Ben and Sophie danced around the room. (slowly)

3 The children spoke English. (well)

4 Amy closed the door. (quietly)

5 Dad drove the car into the garage. (carefully)

6 Tom agreed to help Jack in the test. (stupidly)

7 Ben read the letter that was lying on the table. (quickly)

8 Jack's daughters always work for school. (hard)

9 The children played their music. (loudly)

10 Tom behaved at the family party. (badly)

11 The home crowd cheered when their team scored the winning goal. (happily)

12 The teacher explained the rules for indirect speech to the children. (patiently)

Adjektive und Adverbien

Die Stellung von Adverbien – Adverbiale Bestimmungen des Ortes und der Zeit

Das ist wichtig!

Schau dir diese Beispiele an:

1 The children went home **after tea**.
2 **After tea** the children went home.

> **!Merke**
> 1 Die **Zeitangabe** steht normalerweise am **Satzende** – immer **hinter der Ortsangabe** (Ort vor Zeit).
> 2 Die Zeitangabe kann **zur Betonung** aber auch am **Satzanfang** stehen.

Übung 8

Put these sentence parts in the right order.

1 to bed/last night/went/we/early

   Last night

2 are going/to the concert/they/on Friday

   They

3 did you get/what time/this morning/to school?

4 meet/at 2 pm/outside the school gates I/I'll/you

5 has invited/to his party/on Saturday/us/Tim

6 on the beach/at the weekend/were/a lot of people/there

Die Stellung von Adverbien – Adverbiale Bestimmungen des Ortes und der Zeit

Übung 9

Where do these words belong?

1 Kate met her boyfriend ⬇ six months ago. (on the train)

2 We go to the cinema at the weekends. (often)

3 Sophie did her homework in her bedroom. (after lunch)

4 The hockey team won the match. (easily)

5 Kate sang at the concert on Friday. (beautifully)

6 Be polite to your teachers. (always)

7 I have been to the USA. (never)

8 Sophie has to help her mother at home. (usually)

9 He can remember names. (1 never, 2 well)

10 They speak English. (1 hardly ever, 2 at home)

Das kann ich hier üben!	Das kann ich jetzt!			
		😊	😐	☹
Ich kenne den Unterschied zwischen Adjektiven und Adverbien.		☐	☐	☐
Ich beherrsche den Gebrauch von Adjektiven nach Zustandsverben.		☐	☐	☐
Die Verwendung von Partizipien als Adjektive habe ich verstanden.		☐	☐	☐
Mit der Stellung der Adverbien der Häufigkeit, der Adverbien der Art und Weise und der Adverbialen des Ortes und der Zeit kenne ich mich aus.		☐	☐	☐

Anhang: Weitere Ausdrücke und Verbindungen, die das *gerund* erfordern

Verben

to admit (zugeben); *to avoid* (vermeiden); *to begin* (anfangen); *can't help* (nichts dafür können); *can't stand* (nicht ausstehen können); *to consider* (sich überlegen); *to continue* (fortfahren); *to deny* (abstreiten); *to enjoy* (Spaß haben, mögen, gefallen); *to fancy* (Lust haben); *to finish* (mit etwas fertig werden/sein); *to hate* (hassen); *to imagine* (sich vorstellen); *to like* (mögen, etwas gern tun); *to mean* (bedeuten); *to mind* (dagegen sein); *to regret* (bedauern, dass man etwas getan hat); *to practise* (üben); *to remember* (sich erinnern); *to risk* (riskieren); *to spend (time)* (Zeit verbringen mit); *to start* (anfangen); *to stop* (aufhören); *to suggest* (vorschlagen); *to understand* (verstehen).

Verb-Präposition-Verbindungen

to apologize (to somebody) **for** (sich (bei jemandem entschuldigen für); *to believe* **in** (glauben an); *to carry* **on** (weiter machen); *to complain* **about** (sich beklagen/beschweren über); *to concentrate* **on** (sich konzentrieren auf); *to dream* **of/about** (träumen von); *to feel* **like** (Lust haben); *to get used* **to** (sich gewöhnen an); *to give* **up** (aufgeben); *to go* **on** (weitermachen mit dem gleichen); *to insist* **on** (bestehen auf); *to keep* **on** (etwas immer wieder tun); *to look forward* **to** (sich freuen auf); *to prevent somebody* **from** (jemanden abhalten von); *to succeed* **in** (gelingen); *to speak (talk)* **of/about** (sprechen von/über); *to think* **of/about** (überlegen); *to worry* **about** (sich Sorgen machen).

Adjektiv-Präposition-Verbindungen

to be afraid **of** (Angst haben vor); *to be annoyed (angry)* **at/about** (verärgert sein, weil); *to be ashamed* **of** (sich schämen für); *to be crazy* **about** (verrückt sein nach); *to be delighted* **at/about** (erfreut sein über); *to be famous* **for** (berühmt sein für); *to be fed up* **with** (etwas satt haben); *to be fond* **of** (etwas gern tun); *to be frightened* **of** (Angst haben vor); *to be good/bad* **at** (gut/schlecht sein in); *to be happy/pleased* **about** (sich freuen über); *to be interested* **in** (sich interessieren für); *to be keen* **on** (etwas gern bzw. mit Begeisterung tun); *to be nervous* **about** (Angst haben vor); *to be proud* **of** (stolz sein auf); *to be tired* **of** (etwas satt haben); *to be used* **to** (etwas gewohnt sein); *to be worried* **about** (besorgt sein wegen).

Nomen-Präposition-Verbindungen

chance **of** (Chance, Möglichkeit, etwas zu tun); *to be in danger* **of** (Gefahr laufen); *difficulty (in)* (Schwierigkeiten); *the disadvantage* **of** (der Nachteil von); *experience* **of** (Erfahrung mit); *for fear* **of** (aus Angst, dass); *hope* **of** (Hoffnung); *the idea/thought* **of** (der Gedanke daran); *intention* **of** (die Absicht, etwas zu tun); *the reason* **for** (der Grund, weshalb); *way(s)* **of** (Art/Methode, etwas zu tun).

Bestimmte Ausdrücke

How about/What about (Wie wäre es mit); *it's no good/use* (es hat keinen Zweck/Sinn); *it's worth* (es lohnt sich); *there's no point in* (es hat keinen Zweck/Sinn).

Konjunktionen

after (nachdem); *before* (bevor); *when* (als); *although* (obwohl); *apart from* (abgesehen von); *by* (indem); *without* (ohne); *instead of* (anstatt zu).

Lösungen

Das *simple present* und das *present progressive*

Übung 1

Jack **is** very lazy. He **never walks** anywhere. His mother **always drives** him to school in the mornings and at 4 o'clock, when school **ends**, she **picks** him up again. After school Jack **doesn't often do** his homework, he **usually plays** a game on his computer instead, or he **lies** on his bed and **reads** a magazine. Then after tea, when the soaps **start**, you can always find him in the living room, where he **watches** TV until he **falls** asleep.
The weekends are just the same. It's Saturday afternoon now. And what **is Jack doing**? **Is he playing** football with his friends? No, of course not. He **is sitting** on the sofa in the living room and he **is watching** a DVD.

Übung 2

1. I **don't know** how old Jane is. I **think** she is 14, but I'm not sure.
2. No sorry, I can't lend you my dictionary. I**'m using** it myself at the moment.
3. No sorry, I can't lend you my dictionary. I **need** it myself at the moment.
4. Can I call you back in 10 minutes? We **are having** lunch right now.
5. I'm sorry, I **don't understand** what you **are trying** to tell me.
6. What's the matter with Amy? She **doesn't look** very happy.
7. Ben **is thinking** of selling his computer, but he **doesn't think** he will get much money for it.

Übung 3

Robbie: Who **usually takes** the dog for a walk?
Toby: Well, my mother **always takes** him in the mornings when I**'m** at school and she **sometimes takes** him in the afternoons, too, when I **don't have** time.
Robbie: And who **is taking** him today?
Toby: I am. **Do you want to** come with me?
Robbie: I'm sorry I can't. I**'m meeting** Jack in town at 5.30. We **are going** to the cinema together.
Toby: That **sounds** like a good idea. Can I come with you? The dog **only needs** a short walk today.
Robbie: OK. Let's meet at the bus stop at 5 pm. But don't be late. The bus **leaves** at five past and it **usually runs** on time.
Toby: Great! See you then.

Das *simple past* und das *past progressive*

Zukünftiges im Englischen ausdrücken
Übung 1

1. It's Jack's birthday on Saturday. He will be 14, so he **is going to invite** 14 friends to a sleepover.
2. "What are your plans for this evening?" – "I **'m going to do** my homework and then I **'m going to watch** TV."
3. "I don't know if I can come to your party. I **'ll let** you know by tomorrow."
4. I feel terrible. I think I **'m going to be** sick.
5. I feel terrible. I think I **'ll go and lie down** for a while.
6. Tim: We need some food for the party.
   Mum: OK. I **'ll make** some sandwiches for you.
7. Dad: Tim needs some food for the party.
   Mum: Yes, I know. I **'m going to make** some sandwiches for him.

Übung 2

2. We **will only go** away for Christmas if we **find** a cheap hotel.
3. When Mark **goes** to England next summer, he **isn't going to speak** a word of German for two weeks.
4. "I **'m not going to speak** to Amy again until she **apologizes** for what she said about me."
5. "Mum, I promise that I´ll **tidy** my room before I **go** to bed."
6. "Jack, your room is in such a mess!" – "I know. I **'m going to tidy** it before I **go** to bed."
7. "If I **go out** before you **get home**, I´ll **leave** a message for you on the kitchen table."
8. Kate: "Do you think you **will be allowed to** stay the night at my house on Friday?"
   Jenny: "I'm not sure. I **'ll ask** my mother when I **get** home and I **'ll phone** you this evening."
9. Tom **will be** 25 when he **gets married** next year, but he **is going to wait** until he **is** 30 before he **has** children.

Das *simple past* und das *past progressive*
Übung 1

1. While Jenny **was staying** with her cousin in Vancouver last summer, they **went on** a movie tour of the city and they **saw** a lot of famous actors.

Lösungen

2   Julian **was running** up the escalator when suddenly he **tripped** and **fell**. Luckily, he **didn't hurt** himself very badly.
3   When Amy **went** on an exchange visit to Germany last year, she **spoke** German every day.
4   Harry **cut** his finger when he **was peeling** the potatoes. (*hier:* when = während)
5   The pupils **started** rehearsing for the school play at 4 pm. Five hours later they **were still rehearsing**.
6   When Lisa first **met** Jenny, she **didn't like** her. She **thought** she was arrogant.
7   I'm sorry, I **didn't hear** what you said. I **was just thinking** about something else.
8   What **was Tom wearing** when he left the house this morning?
9   What **did Tom wear** to the party yesterday?

S. 16 Übung 2

When the teacher **came** into the classroom, everybody **was doing** something. Jack **was reading** a comic. Tim **was writing** a note to his girlfriend. William and Harry **were copying** their homework from Ben. The twins **were chatting** on their mobile phones. Lucy **was singing** her favourite song. Some of the pupils **were dancing** around the desks and others **were laughing** and **clapping** their hands. Nobody **was getting** ready for the lesson. But as soon as they **saw** the teacher, everything suddenly **went** quiet. The pupils quickly **sat down** at their desks, **opened** their books and **began** to work.

S. 17 Übung 3

1   The radio was on but nobody **was listening**.
2   We weren't driving very fast when the accident **happened**.
3   It **was getting** dark, so we turned the lights on.
4   When Tom's dad read his report, he **became/got** angry.
5   Amy **was eating** a piece of cake when the phone rang.
6   For tea Amy **ate** two pieces of chocolate cake.
7   When I saw Sophie last, she **was sitting** in the cafeteria.
8   When I arrived at the cafeteria, Tom wasn't there. So I **sat down** and **waited** for him.
9   **Were you sleeping** when the phone rang?
10 **Did you sleep** at Tom's house last night?

Das *simple past* und das *present perfect* verglichen

Übung 1

1. Ben can't go swimming. He **has broken** his arm.
2. Ben can't go swimming. He **broke** his arm yesterday.
3. Tom **finished** his German homework before tea, but he **hasn't finished** his Maths homework yet.
4. Kate **was born** in South Africa but her parents **moved** to Britain when she **was** only one year old. So she **has spent** most of her life there.
5. Mrs Wallace is the best English teacher we **have ever had**. The teacher we **had** last year **wasn't** very good. We **didn't learn** much with her.
6. **Have you been** to the new Italian restaurant that **has just opened** in Main St? – Yes, I have. I **had** lunch there last week. It **was** very good.

Übung 2

1. Mr Winter **started** work at 8 o'clock this morning.
2. Mr Winter **has been** at the office since 8 o'clock this morning.
3. How's Lucy? – I really don't know. I **haven't seen** her for a long time. But the last time I **spoke** to her she was fine.
4. Tom **met** his girlfriend soon after he **moved** to San Diego.
5. Tom **has known** his girlfriend since he **moved** to San Diego.
6. Ben last **saw** his grandparents at Christmas.
7. Ben **hasn't seen** his grandparents since Christmas.
8. Where's Mum? – She **has gone** shopping. She **left** the house about five minutes ago.
9. The phone bill **has gone down** since Daniel **broke up** with his girlfriend.
10. The phone bill **has gone down** since Daniel **has had to** pay for all his own calls.

Übung 3

1. Is it the band's first concert in Germany or **have they played** here before?
2. Lily is in the living room. – Oh! When **did she arrive**? Why **didn't you tell** me that she was here?
3. How long **did it take** you to do your homework yesterday?
4. How long **have you been** at your school?
5. Amy: I like your new jacket. Where **did you buy** it?
   Ellie: At the new boutique in the shopping mall. **Have you ever been** there?
6. Please don't pull the dog's tail. How many times **have I told** you that he doesn't like it.

Lösungen

Das *present perfect progressive*

Übung 1

3 **since** yesterday
4 **since** last summer
5 **for** two minutes
6 **for** years
7 **since** Christmas
8 **for** a long time
9 **since** the beginning of the year
10 **for** ages
11 **since** he was little
12 **for** as long as I can remember

Übung 2

2 Jenny has been learning German …
   a) **for** two years.　　　　b) **since** Year 7.
3 The girls have been rehearsing for their school play …
   a) **since** the beginning of the year.　　b) **for** two months.
4 Jack has got a new girlfriend. He has been going out with her …
   a) **since** last Wednesday.　　b) **for** almost a week.
5 Katie has been singing with the band …
   a) **for** as long as I can remember.　　b) **since** 2005.
6 They have been touring the country …
   a) **since** August.　　　　b) **for** three months.

Übung 3

2 Julia **has been researching** her project on the Internet **all** afternoon.
3 Harry and Tom **have been sitting** in front of the TV **since** they got home from school.
4 My uncle and aunt **have been going** to Thailand for their holidays **for** as long as I can remember.
5 The two girls **have been having** riding lessons **since** they were little.
6 Sophie **has been singing** in the school choir **since** she was ten years old.
7 Grandma **has been living** next door to us **since** Grandpa died.
8 The two girls **have been gossiping** on the phone **all** morning.
9 Tom **has been going out** with his girlfriend **since** they met on holiday last year.
10 Kate **has been texting** me every single day **for** the last six months.

Übung 4

2 I'm **waiting** for a Number 9 bus into town. I **have been waiting** for almost half an hour now.
3 The neighbours **are having** another party on Saturday. They **have been having** parties all summer.

Das present perfect simple und das present perfect progressive verglichen

4 "Please don't disturb Tom." – "Why? What **is he doing**?" – "He **is trying** to do his homework but he **isn't getting** on very well with it."
5 "I haven't seen you for a long time. What **have you been doing**?" – "Oh, you know me. I **have been keeping** myself busy."

Das *present perfect simple* und das *present perfect progressive* verglichen

Übung 1
S. 27

1 You **have been watching** TV for three hours now. Please turn the TV off now.
2 Jack is always late. I don't think he **has ever arrived** anywhere on time.
3 The weather is terrible. It **has been raining** all week.
4 The film was very funny. I **have never laughed** so much in my life.
5 Kate **has made** her bed and she **has put** her dirty clothes in the washing, but she **hasn't tidied** her desk yet.
6 You **have been playing** on the Wii all evening. Can't you do something else now?
7 We're having a garden party on Saturday. We **have invited** 50 people.
8 I think Kate should go and see a doctor. She **has been coughing** all week.
9 Oh Lucy, there you are at last. I **have been trying** to phone you <u>all day</u>.
10 Oh Lucy, there you are at last. I **have tried** to phone you at least <u>ten times</u> today.

Übung 2
S. 28

1 Ben **has wanted** to become an actor **since** he was in his first school play.
2 Lucy and Olivia **have been e-mailing** each other **since** they met on holiday last year.
3 Our English teacher is ill at the moment. She **hasn't been** at school **since** last week.
4 The band **have had** a lot of success **since** their first hit in 2005.
5 They **have been raising** money for charity **for** as long as I can remember.
6 How long **have the children been practising (practicing)** for the school concert?
7 How long **has Amy been** a fan of hip hop music?
8 Mum: Ben, you **have been** at home for three hours now. What **have you been doing** all this time?
    Ben: I **have been texting** my friends, I **have been surfing** the Internet, I **have been playing** on the Wii. And yes, Mum, you are right again. I **haven't started** to do my homework yet.
9 The teacher **has been talking about** the present perfect for two weeks now, but not all the pupils **have understood** it yet. And what about you? **Have you understood** it yet?

Lösungen

Das *past perfect simple* und das *past perfect progressive* verglichen

S. 31 Übung 1

3 Tim couldn't go swimming last Saturday because he **had** a cold.
4 Tim couldn't play football last Saturday because he **had broken** a bone in his foot.
5 I couldn't open the door because I **didn't have** a key.
6 I couldn't open the door because I **had lost** my key.
7 Jack was surprised when Tom **invited** him to his party because he **hadn't heard** from him for a long time.
8 Jack was surprised when Tom **invited** him to his party because he **thought** he **didn't like** him.

S. 32 Übung 2

1 Ben didn't want to go to the cinema again. He **had already seen** the film twice.
2 The boys **had only been playing** football in the park for about ten minutes when it started to rain.
3 Katie wasn't sure if she wanted to audition for a role in the school play. She **hadn't made up** her mind.
4 After she **had had** toothache for about a week, Kate went to see the dentist.
5 The singer was exhausted because she **had been touring** the country for two months. (= *wie lange*)
6 The singer was exhausted because she **had given** ten concerts in the last two months. (= *wie viel*)

S. 32 Übung 3

When Katie arrived at the cafeteria, Daniel **had already been waiting** for twenty minutes. After they **had had** something to eat and drink, they decided to go to the park to play mini-golf.
They **had been playing** mini-golf for about half an hour when Katie asked Daniel if he **had noticed** that a man **had been watching** them ever since they **had arrived** there. When Daniel said that he **had seen** him at the cafeteria and was sure that he **had followed** them to the park, Katie was worried. After they **had finished** the game, which Katie won easily, they walked quickly back to town. They **had only been looking** at the computer games in a large department store for about five minutes when suddenly they saw him again. He **had followed** them back to town. Daniel and Katie had no idea who he was. They **had never seen** him before.

Modale Hilfsverben mit dem Infinitiv Präsens und dem Infinitiv Perfekt

Übung 1

2. We <u>might have been</u> late.
3. They <u>must have known</u> the truth.
4. We <u>ought to have left</u> before lunch.
5. Tom <u>can't have said</u> that.
6. Jack <u>could have flown</u> to New York.
7. You <u>needn't have done</u> that.

Übung 2

3. The lights were on and I could hear voices, so they must **have been** at home.
4. You shouldn't **have told** Kate what I said. She will be angry with me now.
5. We ought to **leave** now. It's getting late.
6. If they had told you the truth, what would you **have done**?
7. We had no idea that the river was inhabited by crocodiles. The locals could **have warned** us not to swim there.

Übung 3

2. How **should Amy have reacted?**
3. **Who could I have asked?**
4. **Why must Tom have known?**
5. **Where can I have put my shoes?**

Übung 4

1. Bringing up three children on her own **must have been difficult.**
2. Ben isn't home yet. **He may have missed the bus.**
3. We've got plenty of time, so you **needn't/don't have to hurry.**
4. Amy looks very happy. She **must have got a good mark in her test.**

Übung 5

1. Tom must have seen me.
2. **Ben can't have gone home.**

Lösungen

3 I should have called a doctor.
4 You could have asked me.
5 They may/might have been afraid.
6 What could I have said?
7 You could have texted me./You could have sent me a text message.
8 You needn't have waited.
9 We could have eaten something at the restaurant.

Bedingungssätze vom Typ I, II und III

S. 39 ### Übung 1

1 If Tom **goes** to bed late, he **will feel** tired tomorrow.
2 If he **is** tired tomorrow he **won't be able to** concentrate in class.
3 If he **doesn't concentrate** in class, he **won't understand** what the teacher is talking about and he **won't be able to** do his homework.
4 If he **doesn't do** his homework again, he **will get** into trouble and his teacher **will give** him another bad mark.
5 If he **gets** another bad mark, his parents **won't be** happy and he **will be grounded**.
6 If Tom **is grounded**, he **won't be** happy either because he **won't be able to** meet his new girlfriend.

S. 40 ### Übung 2

1 If Katie **had** a dog, she **would take** him for a walk every day.
2 If she **took** him for a walk every day, she **wouldn't waste** so much time watching TV.
3 If she **didn't waste** so much time watching TV, she **would probably do** better at school.
4 If she **did** better at school, she **would enjoy** it more and she **would have** more self-confidence.
5 If she **had** more self-confidence, the other children **wouldn't bully** her and she **would be** more popular.
6 If she **were** more popular, she **would be** much happier and she **would enjoy** life more.
7 If she **enjoyed** life more, she **wouldn't be** so bad-tempered.
8 So if I **were** Katie's parents, I **would get** her a dog.

Bedingungssätze vom Typ I, II und III

Übung 3

1. If my mother **hadn't met** your mother yesterday, she **would never have found out** about the party.
2. If she **hadn't found out** about the party, I **wouldn't have been grounded**.
3. If I **hadn't been grounded**, I **would have been allowed to** go to the disco.
4. If I **had been allowed to** go to the disco, I **would have gone** with Amy.
5. I'm sure Amy **would have said** "Yes" if I **had asked** her to go with me.
6. So, you see, if you **hadn't told** your mother about the party and she **hadn't met** my mother yesterday, I **would have been able to** go to the disco with Amy and I **would have been** the happiest person alive and this disaster in my life **would never have happened**.

Übung 4

1. I'll lend you my new DVD if you **promise** to give it back to me tomorrow.
2. If we had a garden, we **would grow** our own vegetables.
3. I**'ll send** you a text message if I miss the train.
4. The dog wouldn't be so fat if he **got** more exercise.
5. Dad wouldn't have got a parking ticket if he **hadn't parked** the car in a no-parking zone.
6. If we didn't have a car, we **would have to** go by train.
7. If my mother had studied French instead of German at university, she **would never have met** my father.
8. I wouldn't have been late for school this morning if I **hadn't forgotten** to set my alarm clock.
9. The holiday won't be too expensive if we **stay** at youth hostels.
10. If I had known that it was a secret, I **wouldn't have told** anybody.
11. If we book the holiday on the Internet, **will it make** a difference in price?

Übung 5

1. The Browns aren't poor. If they **were** poor, they **wouldn't be able to** send their children to private schools.
2. My parents are thinking of emigrating to Australia, but we **will only move** there if my father **finds** a good job.
3. Why didn't you ask Dad if you could borrow his camera? If you **had asked** him, I'm sure he **would have lent** it to you.
4. That potato salad has been in the sun too long. I **wouldn't eat** it if I **were** you.
5. I'm glad that we live in a town. If we **lived** in the country, we **would have to** travel miles to reach the nearest shops.

Lösungen

6 The village was difficult to find. If we **hadn't had** a satnav, he **would never have found** it.

Übung 6 (S. 44)

2 If you **don't keep** your dog on a lead, **he may/might chase** the sheep in the fields.
3 If you **are** hungry, please **help** yourselves to the biscuits.
4 You **must post** the birthday card today if you **want** it to arrive on time.
5 You **mustn't be** rude to people if you **want** them to help you.
6 That restaurant **can't be** any good if nobody ever **eats** there.
7 You **needn't meet** us at the airport if you **don't have** time. We can take the train.
8 If you **need** any help, **don't be** afraid to ask me.
9 If you **chat** to somebody online who you don't know, you **should never tell** him/her your real name.

Übung 7 (S. 45)

1 If you had gone to bed earlier last night, you **wouldn't be** tired today.
2 If Mum hadn't forgotten to close all the windows, we **wouldn't have had to** turn back.
3 If you had had a drink at the restaurant, you **wouldn't be** thirsty now.
4 If we had been able to get a flight, we **would have spent** the weekend in New York.
5 If Amy had learnt to dance when she was young, she **could be** a star today.
6 If Ruby hadn't read the problem page in her favourite teen magazine, she **wouldn't have known** how to react to the bullies at her school.
7 If you had done your homework earlier, you **would be able to** watch TV now.
8 If the police had arrived sooner, they **might have caught** the burglars.

Übung 8 (S. 46)

1 **They would be very disappointed if they didn't win the competition.**
2 **If you had asked me, I would have helped you.**
3 **If you had had breakfast, you wouldn't be hungry now.**
4 **If the man had spoken a bit more slowly, I might have understood him.**
5 **If you saw Tom now, you would get a shock.**
6 **If I don't feel better tomorrow, I will go to the doctor's./If I don't feel better tomorrow, I will go and see a doctor.**
7 What would you have done if the bus hadn't come?

Alle Zeitformen auf einen Blick

Übung 1

Mum: What are your plans for this evening?
Ellie: I**'m going** to the cinema with Harry. We **are meeting** outside the Odeon at 7.30. The film **starts** at 8.
Mum: And what time **does it finish**?
Ellie: No idea, but I'm sure it **won't be** late.

Übung 2

Ben: What **are you doing**, Harry?
Harry: I**'m watching** those workmen over there. In fact, I **have been watching** them for over three hours now and they **haven't even started** to work yet.

Übung 3

Jack **is learning** to drive now. He **has been having** driving lessons since Christmas. He **has had** 20 lessons so far. He **is going to take/is taking** his driving test on Thursday.

Übung 4

Lily: What **are you doing** this evening?
Emily: I**'m going** to Paris for the weekend. My parents **are taking** me to Disneyland.
Lily: Lucky you! How **are you getting** there?
Emily: We **are flying**. Our flight **leaves** at 9 pm.
Lily: I**'ll ask** my mum if she can take you to the airport if you **like**.
Emily: No, it's OK, thanks. My brother **is driving/is going to drive** us.

Übung 5

1. When Ellie arrived at the cinema, Jack **was waiting for** her.
2. When Ellie arrived at the cinema, Jack **had been waiting for** her for twenty minutes.
3. I went into the shop because I **was looking for** a birthday present for my best friend.
4. I went into the shop because I **knew** the shop assistants there.
5. I went into the shop because I **had seen** their advertisement in the newspaper.
6. I woke up at 6 o'clock this morning because my dog **was barking** loudly.

Lösungen

7 I woke up at 6 o'clock this morning, looked at the clock and then **went back** to sleep again.
8 I woke up at 6 o'clock this morning because I **was** cold. I **had forgotten** to shut the window.
9 The fans reacted very badly when they **heard** that the band **wanted** to split up.
10 The fans reacted very badly when they **heard** that the band **had decided** to split up.

Übung 6 — S. 51

The Titanic **has been lying** on the bottom of the ocean since 1912. It **sank** on its maiden voyage from Southampton to New York. When the ship **hit** the ice-berg, the passengers and the crew **didn't panic** at first. By the time they **realized** that the ship **was sinking**, it was too late. Most of the lifeboats **had already left** half-full. 1,503 people **lost** their lives in the tragedy.

Übung 7 — S. 51

When I **got** home from work on Monday, I **opened** the front door and **stepped** into a pool of water which **was coming** out from under the kitchen door. The hose on my dish-washer **had burst**. The engineer **promised** to come and mend it straightaway, but that **was** four days ago and I **haven't heard** from him since.

Übung 8 — S. 52

I **was diving** off the coast of Florida when I **came across** George, the resident shark. The diving instructor **had warned** me about him, so, of course, I **knew** immediately that he **was** harmless. But in that terrifying moment as he **was swimming** directly towards me, I suddenly **began** to wonder whether he **knew** that, too.

Übung 9 — S. 52

J. K. Rowling **began** her writing life as a single mother who **was living** on state benefits. But soon the magical characters that she **created** in her Harry Potter books **shot** her to international stardom and by 2001 she **had become** the highest-paid woman in Britain. Yet despite her enormous success, J. K. Rowling **has kept** her feet firmly on the ground. Today, she **lives** in Scotland with her second husband, who **is** a doctor.

Alle Zeitformen auf einen Blick

Übung 10

Amy: Lucy, there you are at last! Where **have you been**? I **have been waiting** for you for fifteen minutes. We **arranged** to meet here at 3 o'clock, remember?

Lucy: Oh I'm sorry. I **was just passing** that new boutique that **has just opened** on the corner when I **saw** a really nice T-shirt in the window. I **have been looking for** one like that for weeks, so I **thought** I must just go in and try it on. Look, here it is. What **do you think** of it?

Amy: It **looks** great. You **won't believe** it but I **bought** exactly the same T-shirt from that same shop yesterday.

Übung 11

Every month I **send** an e-mail to my e-friend in England. Last week I **told** her about our class trip to Freiburg. We all **enjoyed** it so much and it **was** great to have a whole week without any lessons!
At the moment I**'m revising** for our next English test. We **are having** it on Friday. I **haven't learned** so much for a long time and I hope it **won't be** too difficult. I **have been sitting** at my desk since 5 o'clock. I couldn't start working before because I **had forgotten** to take my front door key with me, so I **had to** wait for my parents to come home from work first. But as soon as I **had finished** tea, I **went** up to my room. It **is** 8 o'clock now, so that means I **have been working** for three hours. I **think** I**'ll go** to bed. I **have done** enough for today.

Übung 12

Two owls or two twits? (*Zwei Eulen oder zwei Trottel?*)
Mr Brown has been keen on owls since childhood, so he **was** very excited one day last week when he **heard** that some owls **were building/had built** their nest in the woods nearby.
That night he **decided** to try his luck. At 11 pm he **went** out into his garden and **began** to hoot. "Twit…to…woo," he **called**. "Twit…to…woo," came the immediate reply. Mr Brown **couldn't believe** it. So the next night he **tried** again and then every night for a week, and each night the same thing **happened**. Mr Brown **was** amazed and his wife **was** amazed, too, that is, until she **met** Mrs Fry at a coffee morning one day.
Mrs Brown **had just finished** telling the story when Mrs Fry said, "That's funny. My husband **likes** owls, too, and he **has been going** out at 11 pm for months now to hoot to them as well, but it **was** just last week that an owl suddenly **began** to hoot back at him."

Lösungen

Das Gerundium (*gerund*)

Übung 1 (S. 56)

1 **Walking to school** is good for you.
2 **Shopping** in New York is really great, but …
3 … **driving in the city** is a nightmare.
4 **Tidying my room** isn't one of my hobbies.
5 **Sitting at home all day** is terribly boring.

Übung 2 (S. 57)

Lily's hobbies are watching DVDs, **playing on the Wii**, reading, playing table-tennis, listening to CDs, watching TV, **going shopping** and **going to the cinema**.

Übung 3 (S. 58)

2 My dad **didn't <u>like learning</u>** Latin when he was at school.
3 Luke **<u>loves being</u>** the centre of attention.
4 What do you **<u>enjoy doing</u>** in your free time?
5 Could you ever **<u>imagine living</u>** in New York?
6 Would you **<u>mind waiting</u>** for me?
7 That phone never **<u>stops ringing</u>**.

Übung 4 (S. 59)

1 When Ben moves to New York, he won't miss his teachers, but he **will miss being** with his friends.
2 Amy decided to do her homework because she didn't want **to risk getting** into trouble again.
3 You needn't pick me up from the airport. I don't **mind catching** the train.
4 Don't worry if you are not successful at first. Just **keep trying**.
5 I gave the magazine to Amy because I **had finished reading** it.
6 When Katie's cousin comes to stay with her in New York, she **will enjoy showing** her around the city.

Übung 5 (S. 60)

2 Sophie is looking forward **to moving** to France soon.
3 Do your best and don't worry **about making** mistakes.
4 A lot of teenagers dream **of becoming** famous.
5 I don't feel **like going** out this evening.
6 The girls talked **about auditioning** for a talent show.

Das Gerundium (*gerund*)

7   Tom was lazy. He never believed **in working** hard.
8   Ben didn't care **about losing** the tennis match.

Übung 6

2   Claudia isn't afraid **of being** in the house on her own.
3   Jack's mother is tired **of asking** him to tidy his room.
4   I'm very bad **at singing**.
5   Are you worried **about going** to the dentist's tomorrow?
6   I'm not crazy **about skiing**.
7   Tom has never been interested **in playing** football.
8   We aren't used **to getting up** early on Sundays.
9   Some people are just famous **for being** famous.
10 Ben was angry **about being dropped** from the football team.

Übung 7

2   Don't tell Kate. She **isn't good at** keeping secrets.
3   Tom wants to leave now. He **is worried about/afraid of** missing his flight.
4   Why can you never be on time? I'**m tired of** having to wait for you all the time.
5   I didn't say anything because I **was afraid of** hurting his feelings.
6   Most teenagers today **are interested in** learning more about how to protect the environment.
7   Don't become a teacher if you **aren't interested in/aren't good at** working with children.

Übung 8

2   What are our chances **of winning the World Cup**?
3   Do you have any **experience of working with children**?
4   Many immigrants went to America **in the hope of leading a better life**.

Übung 9

1   I'm afraid there isn't much **hope/chance of** finding the little girl alive.
2   The **advantage of** living close to your school is that you don't have to get up early in the morning.
3   The **reason for** having games lessons at school is so that children get some exercise.
4   The **thought of/idea of** having to sing in front of an audience of millions filled me with fear.

Lösungen

Übung 10

2 I can't stand **them lying** to **me**.
3 I don't mind **you borrowing** my mobile.
4 Ben's mother **is looking forward to him coming** home for Christmas.
5 My mother is always **nervous about me going** out on my own at night.
6 Sarah's mother **is very proud of her being** able to speak three languages fluently.

Übung 11

2 The book is really interesting. **It's worth reading**.
3 The weather is so nice. **How about going for a walk**?
4 The computer was so old that **it wasn't worth repairing**.
5 The matter was so unimportant that there **was no point in talking about** it.
6 It**'s no use offering** him advice. He never listens anyway.
7 There**'s no point in offering** him advice. He never listens anyway.

Übung 12

2 Think carefully about what you want to say **before phoning** him.
3 Jack left the party **without saying** thank-you.
4 **After finishing** her breakfast, Ellie left the house.
5 **After hearing** about the accident, Kate rushed to hospital.
6 We drove all the way to Hamburg **without** even **stopping** for lunch.
7 The film star waved to the crowd **before driving** away in a large black car.

Übung 13

Amy's Diary

Dear Diary,
They did it again. They all laughed at me again in class. Tim wrote some stupid story about a girl with red hair, and then everybody looked at me and **started laughing**.
Why **do they keep (on) doing** that? Why **do they keep (on) making fun of** my red hair? Why **must they keep calling** me Ginger? My name is Amy, not Ginger! There was a time when I actually **enjoyed going** to school. Well, maybe not exactly enjoy, but at least I **didn't mind going** to school. But not now. Not since that horrible Tim joined the class and **started bullying** me.
Most days I **don't** even **feel like getting** out of bed. Mum says I **should stop worrying** about stupid people like Tim. But that's easy to say, isn't it? How **can I**

stop worrying when he makes my life such hell? I **have** even **thought of (about) dyeing** my hair black. But Mum says if I do that, then the bullies will win.
Dear Diary, help me, please!

Der Infinitiv
Übung 1

2   I don't know **who to ask.**
3   Tom has no idea **how to behave**.
4   The teacher showed the children **where to go** in an emergency.
5   Ellie isn't sure **what to do** when she arrives in New York.
6   Daniel is wondering **whether to buy** a new mobile phone or not.
7   Amy isn't sure **which** trousers **to wear** to the party.
8   Daniel hasn't decided **whether to go** by bus or by train.

Übung 2

Mum: Did you <u>clean</u> the windows?
Daniel: No, Mum. I wasn't sure **which** windows **to clean**.
Mum: Did you <u>look</u> for the front door key that you lost yesterday?
Daniel: No, Mum. I didn't know **where to look**.
Mum: Did you <u>cook</u> the meal?
Daniel: Oh Mum! You know I don't know **how to cook**.
Mum: Did you <u>record</u> my favourite programme?
Daniel: Sorry Mum. I wasn't sure **which** programme **to record**.
Mum: Well, did you <u>do</u> your Maths homework?
Daniel: No Mum. It was so difficult. I had no idea **how to do** it.
Mum: Well, why didn't you <u>phone</u> someone and ask them to help you?
Daniel: I didn't know **who to phone**.

Übung 3

Ben is in New York for the first time. There are so many sights to see that he doesn't know where to go first. He would like to go to the Empire State Building, but he has no idea **how to get** there, so he has to ask somebody.
There are so many people on the street that at first he isn't sure **who to ask**. A friendly woman in a red dress tells him that it is too far to walk and that he should take a cab or go by subway. Ben isn't sure **which** subway **to take**, so he decides to go by cab. When he arrives at the Empire State Building, there is a long queue outside, so now Ben doesn't know **whether to wait** in the queue or **whether to go** somewhere else first. He is really unsure **what to do**.

Lösungen

Übung 4 — S. 71

1. I didn't know **what to say**.
2. Kate knew **who to call/phone**.
3. Jack isn't sure **what to do**.
4. I can't decide **which shoes to wear**.
5. I don't know **how to say** it in English.

Übung 5 — S. 72

2. **The most sensible thing to do** is to say nothing at all.
3. Most pupils did well in the test, but Ben was **the only one to get an A**.
4. Emily was **the last person to arrive** at the party.
5. **The next person to talk** will be sent out of the classroom.
6. You are **the second person to say that**.
7. **The best thing to do** is to keep quiet.

Übung 6 — S. 73

1. I can't answer your question right away. I need some time **to think about** it.
2. There are a lot of things you can do **to protect** the environment.
3. It's my dad's birthday today. We are going out this evening **to celebrate**.
4. I stopped a man in the street **to ask** the way.
5. Ben phoned **to invite** me to the disco on Saturday.

Übung 7 — S. 73

1. I went to the supermarket **to buy** some meat.
2. You will need a knife **to cut** the bread.
3. I went to the travel agency **to get** some brochures.
4. It took Ben ages **to do** his homework yesterday.
5. Nowadays you don't always need a special talent **to become** a star.
6. You need to be creative **to write** a good story.

Übung 8 — S. 74

2. The book was very entertaining and it was also very **easy to read**.
3. It's a very sensitive subject. I think it would probably be **best not to mention** it at all.
4. I was **sorry to hear** about your accident.
5. I think we ought to take the train into town. On Saturdays it is always so **difficult to find** a place to park the car.

Der Infinitiv

6 Let's not wait for the next bus. I'm sure it will be **quicker to walk**.
7 Is it **dangerous to swim** in the sea at this time of year?
8 I was **surprised to see** Jack at the party. I didn't think he would be there.

Übung 9

2 Amy couldn't understand the homework, so I offered **to help** her.
3 What did you do on holiday? – I learned **to sail**.
4 Katie seems **to be** quite happy at her new school.
5 Harry tried **to explain** why he had got home late, but his mother refused **to listen**.
6 Where are the biscuits, Mum? – Oh dear, I forgot **to buy** them.
7 The test was difficult but I managed **to answer** most of the questions.
8 We were all very tired, so we decided **to go** to bed early.
9 Every week millions of people hope **to win** the lottery.
10 Jack promised **not to tell** anyone my secret.

Übung 10

1 I asked Lily where she had been, but she **refused** to tell me.
2 My mother is going to phone my class tutor because she **wants** to know how I am getting on at school now.
3 Hannah left for Scotland this morning. She **promised** to phone me as soon as she arrived.
4 Amy hasn't tidied her room yet, but she definitely **plans** to do it this afternoon.
5 To everyone's amazement Jack **managed** to pass his driver's license yesterday.
6 I don't know the results of the test yet, but I **hope** to get them soon.
7 Jenny **has decided** to join the Drama Club this year.

Übung 11

1 Many immigrants went to America because they **hoped to find** a better life there.
2 When we are in New York next week, of course we **plan to visit** all the usual tourist attractions.
3 The apartment is too small for a family of four, so the Smiths **decided to look for** a larger one.

Lösungen

S. 77 ## Übung 12

1 Amy wanted **to sell her bike**.
2 She wanted **me to sell it**.
3 They would like **to go to the zoo**.
4 They would like **us to go with them**.
5 I didn't expect **to see her** at the party.
6 I didn't expect **her to be** at the party.
7 Can you do your homework on your own or **would you like me to help you**?
8 I didn't take an umbrella with me because I didn't expect **it to rain**.
9 Ben didn't tell Jenny the truth because he didn't want **her to cry**.
10 Have you understood the grammar or **would you like me to explain it to you again**?

S. 78 ## Übung 13

2 Tom **invited me to go** to the disco with him.
3 Katie and Lily's dad **warned them not to be** late for school again.
4 James' mum **advised him to go** to bed early.
5 James' mum **advised him not to go** to bed too late.

S. 79 ## Übung 14

1 **It's best to leave early in the morning.**
2 **It's cheaper to go by car.**
3 **Jenny was the first (person) to arrive.**
4 **Who was the last (person) to leave the room?**
5 **I need some time to think about it.**
6 **They advised him to spend a few weeks at a school in England.**
7 **They want us to lend them some money.**
8 **We warned them not to drink the water.**

Gerundium oder Infinitiv?

S. 81 ## Übung 1

1 I was surprised **to get** Tom's e-mail this morning. I didn't expect **to hear** from him so soon.
2 When I'm on holiday, I enjoy **lying** on the beach and **doing** nothing at all.
3 Teenagers aren't always interested **in learning** for school. Sometimes they have better things **to do**.

Gerundium oder Infinitiv?

4 The children love **living** in the country. They say they wouldn't want **to live** anywhere else. They certainly couldn't imagine **living** in a town.
5 Mum says she is very busy just now but she will be happy **to help** you later.
6 Ben doesn't want **to go** to tennis practice any more. He says he is tired **of playing** tennis.
7 The little girl fell into the pond and was in danger **of drowning**.
8 **Eating** too much junk food is bad for your health.
9 Tim is looking forward **to playing** football on Saturday.
10 Kate was so embarrassed she didn't know where **to look**.
11 Let's take the bus. It's too far **to walk**.

Übung 2

1 The thought **of having to** stay in the house alone didn't frighten Kevin.
2 When she started at her new school, Sophie hoped **to make** new friends very quickly.
3 Jim advised us **not to drive** through the city in the rush-hour.
4 If you are good **at reading** maps, you won't need a navigation system.
5 I decided **to stay** at home last night because I didn't feel well.
6 Grandma says she would love **to visit** us next week.
7 I told him that I wasn't interested **in going** to the party with him, but he kept **(on) asking** me.
8 Are you good **at learning** languages?
9 I know I made a mistake but that really is no reason **for shouting** at me.
10 Jack promised **to be** home before 6 o'clock.

Übung 3

1 Have you decided where **to go** for your holidays?
2 The band are talking **about touring** the country next year.
3 I'm tired **of telling** you not to make so much noise.
4 Jack won the race because he was the first **to cross** the finishing line.
5 Do you enjoy **living** in a small village?
6 Ben left the house without **saying** goodbye.
7 These suitcases are too heavy **to carry**.
8 Sophie's mother told her that **going** on a language course in the summer holidays would help improve her German.
9 Our new teacher finds it difficult **to remember** our names.
10 Our new teacher has difficulty **(in) remembering** our names.

Lösungen

S. 83 — Übung 4

1. Our teacher has been so busy lately that she hasn't had a chance **to correct** our last tests yet.
2. Is there any chance **of getting** tickets for the concert tonight?
3. There is no chance **of catching** our train now. It leaves in 5 minutes.
4. If you had the chance **to travel** anywhere in the world, where would you go?

S. 84 — Übung 5

Would you like to be a celebrity?

In the past, celebrities were people who had become famous because they were exceptionally good (1) **at doing** something like (2) **singing**, (3) **acting** or (4) **playing** a particular sport. Today, however, (5) **having** a special talent no longer seems (6) **to be** a requirement and anyone can become a star. Nowadays just (7) **having** a charismatic personality, (8) **being able to** pose in front of a camera, or simply (9) **being** a WAG (the glamourous wife or girlfriend of a famous footballer) are apparently all the qualifications you need.

So it is hardly surprising that many teenagers now seem (10) **to believe** that even without any particular talent they still have a real chance (11) **of becoming** a star. Thanks to the explosion of TV talent shows, teen magazines and websites such as YouTube and MySpace, for today's teenager the idea (12) **of wanting to be** a celebrity is no longer an impossible dream. The problem today is: Is this dream really still worth (13) **living**? My opinion is that it is not.

Most teenagers associate (14) **being** famous with (15) **having** money, popularity, success and happiness. When they are asked their reasons (16) **for wanting to become** celebrities, they usually mention the money, freebies and the admiration of the fans. For them (17) **being** a celebrity seems such an exciting life. But what they do not realize is that where there are advantages, there are always disadvantages, too. Of course it must be great (18) **to be** rich and famous, but remember that today (19) **becoming** famous is much easier than (20) **staying** famous. Once you are a celebrity you are under constant pressure (21) **to perform** and (22) **to impress** people. Of course money will give you security, but will it bring you happiness? If it does, then why do so many celebrities take drugs?

Of course it must be wonderful (23) **to be** so popular, but how will you know who your true friends are and who you can really trust? Of course it must be fantastic (24) **to see** yourself on the front cover of the glossy magazines, but what if they start (25) **to write/writing** stories about you that you don't want other people (26) **to hear**? And what if they write lies about you? Of course it must be fun when people stop you in the street (27) **to ask** you for your autograph,

Gerundium oder Infinitiv?

(28) **to take** a photo of you on their mobile phone or just (29) **to say** hello. But what if they start (30) **to stalk/stalking** you? As a celebrity your life is no longer your own. Would you like (31) **to live** in a goldfish bowl? – I wouldn't.
(32) **Being** rich and famous may sound great fun, but in reality (33) **being** a celebrity isn't always the glamourous life that people think it is. I would advise anybody (34) **to think** very carefully before (35) **following** this dream.

Übung 6

1. Tom tried **to explain** but his father wouldn't listen.
2. I have stopped **buying** those biscuits because they are too expensive.
3. Did you remember **to take** the bottles to the bottle bank?
4. James tried **following** his father into the music business, but with little success.
5. I didn't have a map, so I had to stop **to ask** someone the way.
6. I remember **meeting** him once before, but I can't remember where.
7. After Ben had finished school, he went on **to study** at university.
8. The shop assistant ignored me completely and went on **talking** to her friend.
9. People often try **to rip off** tourists. You have to be so careful.
10. I'm sorry. I didn't mean **to be** rude.
11. Did you remember **to post** the letter which was on the hall table? – I don't remember you **asking** me to do that.
12. Ben's dad accepted the job in Holland, even though it meant **only being able to** see his family at weekends.
14. Mr Davis could get a job with an oil company, but that would mean **moving** to Texas.
15. The teacher stopped **to think** before **answering** the question.

Übung 7

1. As soon as I realized that he was in trouble, I tried **to help** him.
2. I remember **hearing** Tom say that he would be on holiday in August.
3. We tried **to get** tickets for the concert, but they were all sold out.
4. If you can't hear the TV, why don't you try **turning** up the volume.
5. I've got a terrible headache. Please stop **making** such a noise.
6. You didn't forget **to buy** the milk, did you?
7. I'm very busy. Please stop **disturbing** me.
8. I'll never forget **being stung** by an angry wasp in the garden.
9. If you want to join the orchestra, that will mean **practising** the cello every day.
10. Don't forget **to do** your homework, will you?
11. When new immigrants first arrive in their new homeland, they often only mean **to stay** until they have earned enough money to go back home.

Lösungen

12 Tim wanted **to watch** TV, but Kate wouldn't stop **talking**.
13 Did you remember **to take** your medicine this morning?
14 First Tom worked as a waiter. Then he went on **to become** the manager of the restaurant.
15 Why don't you stop **worrying** about the test and start **to learn/learning** for it instead?

S. 89 — Übung 8

1 I didn't mean <u>to hurt</u> you.
2 Stop <u>annoying</u> me.
3 He went on <u>to explain</u> the rules of the game.
4 We stopped <u>to enjoy</u> the view.
5 Don't forget <u>to bring</u> your camera with you.
6 I will never forget <u>seeing</u> the band live.
7 Did you remember <u>to go</u> to the chemist's for me?
8 Love means never <u>having</u> to say sorry/never <u>having</u> to apologise.
9 I can't remember <u>telling</u> her the story.
10 Try <u>to find out</u> as much information as possible about the Native Americans (Indians).
11 I asked him to be quiet but he went on <u>talking</u>.
12 If I am not at home, try <u>texting</u> me.

Die indirekte Rede

S. 91 — Übung 1

1 Amy told Ellie (that) **they** usually **went** on holiday in August.
2 Tim said (that) **he had done his** homework after lunch.
3 Jack told Ben (that) **he hadn't seen** Tom since Saturday.
4 Sophie **said (that) she would finish** tidying **her** room after tea.
5 Tom **said that he had taken** an aspirin because **he hadn't been** feeling well.
6 Kate **told her sister (that) she was** tired because **she had been working** hard all day.

S. 92 — Übung 2

1 The doctor told Jack (that) **he had to** stay in bed for a week.
2 Mum told Amy that **she should** join a sports club.
3 Sophie told Ellie (that) **she might** be able to help **her**.
4 Lucy said (that) **they ought to** take something to drink with **them**.

Die indirekte Rede

5 Jack said (that) during the holidays <u>he</u> <u>had had to</u> help <u>his</u> uncle on his farm.
6 Ellie told her friends (that) <u>she</u> <u>would</u> tell <u>them</u> tomorrow if <u>they</u> <u>could</u> have the party at <u>her</u> house.

Übung 3

S. 93

a) At the beginning of the lesson the teacher <u>said</u> (that) <u>they</u> <u>were</u> going to practise a listening comprehension. <u>She</u> <u>told</u> the children (that) <u>they</u> <u>would</u> hear the text twice. Before <u>they</u> <u>listened</u> to the text for the first time, <u>they</u> <u>would</u> have one minute to read the questions. <u>She</u> <u>told</u> <u>them</u> that <u>they</u> <u>could</u> start to make notes as soon as <u>they</u> <u>had</u> heard the text once. After <u>they</u> <u>had</u> heard the text for the second time, <u>they</u> <u>had to</u> answer the questions in full sentences. <u>She</u> <u>said</u> (that) the last time <u>they</u> <u>had done</u> a listening comprehension, some of <u>them</u> <u>had</u> only <u>given</u> one-word answers, and (<u>explained that</u>) that <u>was</u> why they <u>had got</u> a bad mark.

b) Paris Hilton <u>said</u> that people <u>thought</u> that they <u>knew</u> <u>her</u>, but they <u>didn't</u>. They <u>read</u> stories in the media and <u>thought</u> that <u>was</u> who <u>she</u> really <u>was</u>. But <u>she</u> <u>was</u> not like <u>her</u> media image at all and <u>she</u> certainly <u>didn't</u> consider <u>herself</u> to be a celebrity. In fact <u>she</u> <u>hated</u> the word. <u>She</u> <u>explained</u> that <u>she</u> <u>was</u> a brand. <u>She</u> <u>had</u> <u>her</u> own perfume, <u>her</u> own make-up, shoes and hotels. <u>She</u> <u>had</u> starred on TV shows, in films and <u>she</u> <u>had</u> made a few records. <u>She</u> <u>said</u> there <u>was</u> nobody else quite like <u>her</u>. <u>She</u> <u>insisted</u> (*behauptete*) that <u>she</u> <u>didn't</u> really pay much attention to the media and <u>said</u> that people <u>could</u> think what they <u>liked</u>. <u>She</u> <u>was</u> living <u>her</u> life, <u>she</u> <u>was</u> having the time of <u>her</u> life and <u>she</u> <u>had</u> never been happier. <u>She</u> <u>hadn't grown</u> up wanting to be a celebrity. <u>She</u> <u>had</u> wanted to be a vet because <u>she</u> <u>loved</u> animals. But <u>she</u> <u>was</u> famous now, and <u>she</u> <u>was</u> very proud of <u>herself</u> because <u>she</u> <u>had</u> achieved so much at such a young age. And that <u>was</u> all that <u>mattered</u> to <u>her</u>.

Übung 4

S. 94

1 Lucy said (that) <u>she</u> <u>was</u> going to cook the lunch <u>that</u> day.
2 Charles told Helen **(that)** <u>he</u> <u>was</u> sure Ellie <u>would</u> be <u>there</u> soon.
3 Mrs Walker said **(that)** <u>she</u> <u>had seen</u> Mrs Dart <u>two days before</u>.
4 **Chloe admitted (that)** <u>she</u> <u>hadn't done</u> her homework <u>the day before</u>.
5 **She promised (that)** <u>she</u> <u>would</u> do it <u>that</u> evening.
6 Mr Carter told his wife **(that)** <u>he</u> <u>was</u> going to Paris <u>the</u> next week.
7 His wife complained **(that)** <u>he</u> <u>had gone</u> there only <u>the week before</u>.
8 She added **(that)** <u>he</u> <u>had</u> promised that <u>she</u> <u>could</u> come with <u>him</u> <u>the</u> next time.

Lösungen

S. 95 Übung 5

2 Amy to Emily on Tuesday: "Kate told me that she is/was going to London **next weekend**."
3 James to a friend (a month later): "When I last spoke to Tom about a month ago, he told me that he had met Daniel **the day before**."
4 Lily to Mum (later): "Lucy told me that Katie is/was coming to see us **tomorrow**."

S. 96 Übung 6

1 The teacher asked Ben and Ellie **why they were laughing**.
2 Dan wanted to know **how much pocket money Tim got**.
3 Ben asked his mother **how long she had been waiting for the bus**.
4 I asked Tom **if he would be able to come to my party**.
5 The shop assistant asked the little boy **where his mother was**.
6 Bill wanted to know **how long Tom had been a fan of Coldplay**.
7 Mrs Bean asked her guest **if she would like a cup of tea**.
8 Julia wanted to know **if Mr Jones drank his tea with milk**.
9 Mum wondered **who had eaten the biscuits**.

S. 97 Übung 7

1 Ben to Jack: "**How much did you pay for the tickets**?"
2 Coach: "**Why weren't you at football practice yesterday**?"
3 Teacher to Ben: "**What do you want to do when you leave school**?"
4 Jack: "**Have you finished reading the magazine, Ben**?"

S. 98 Übung 8

2 Lily <u>asked</u> Hannah <u>to pass</u> her the sugar.
3 Amy's dad <u>advised</u> her <u>never to give</u> anyone her phone number or address when chatting online.
4 Mrs Banks <u>invited</u> her neighbour <u>to come</u> in and have a cup of tea.
5 Tom's dad <u>advised</u> him <u>to go and see</u> the doctor as soon as possible.
6 Jane <u>asked</u> her mum <u>to pick</u> her up from school.
7 The teacher <u>reminded</u> the children <u>to hand in</u> their homework by 9 o'clock.
8 Mum <u>told</u> Lily <u>to tidy</u> her room before her guests arrive<u>d</u> and <u>not to forget</u> to put her socks in the basket.

Die indirekte Rede

9 James **warned** Tim **not to touch** the fence or he **would** get an electric shock.
10 Mary's parents **ordered** her **not to see** that boy again.
11 Jack's mother **told** him **not to worry** if he **got** a bad mark in the test.
12 The teacher **advised** the children **to learn** the rules for indirect speech if they want**ed** to do well in the test.

Übung 9

1 Teacher to the children: "**Stop talking and concentrate on the lesson.**"
2 Aunt Julia to Freddy: "**Come and stay with us whenever you like.**"
3 Dad to Peter: "**Drive slowly and don't drink any alcohol.**"
4 Mum to Kate: "**Can/Could you lay the table, please?**"
5 Teacher to students: "**Don't miss classes or there will be trouble!**"

Übung 10

Sophie's mum <u>asked</u> <u>her</u> what <u>she</u> <u>was</u> going to do when the holidays <u>started</u> <u>the following</u> week.
Sophie <u>replied</u> that <u>she</u> <u>might</u> go to France with Emily or <u>she</u> <u>might</u> go to Italy with Tom. (<u>She</u> <u>said</u>) <u>she</u> <u>hadn't</u> decided yet.
So her mother <u>asked</u> <u>her</u> if <u>she</u> <u>had</u> thought about looking for a holiday job.
Sophie <u>explained</u> that <u>she</u> <u>had</u> tried to find one, but there <u>weren't</u> any.
So then her mum <u>told</u> <u>her</u> that Dixons <u>were</u> looking for a shop assistant in August. <u>She</u> <u>had seen</u> their advert in the newspaper <u>the day before</u>.
She <u>suggested</u> that <u>she</u> <u>rang</u> them and <u>asked</u> if <u>she</u> <u>could</u> come (go) for an interview.
When Sophie <u>replied</u> that <u>she</u> <u>didn't</u> want to work in August because <u>she</u> <u>had been</u> looking forward to relaxing at home …
… her mother <u>said</u> that <u>she</u> <u>had been</u> looking forward to <u>her</u> earning <u>her</u> own pocket money and <u>told</u> <u>her</u> <u>to call</u> them or <u>to send</u> them <u>her</u> application before it <u>was</u> too late.

Übung 11

Amy <u>asked</u> Lily if <u>she</u> <u>had</u> seen the interview with Tom Cruise in "Heaven" <u>that</u> week.
Lily <u>said</u> that <u>she</u> <u>didn't</u> read "Heaven" any more. <u>She</u> <u>told</u> <u>her</u> that <u>she</u> <u>had</u> changed to "Glory" about a month <u>before</u> because <u>she</u> <u>thought</u> it <u>was</u> much

Lösungen

better. It <u>had</u> more articles on celebs, great style tips and good advice. And what <u>was</u> more it <u>had</u> super freebies. <u>That</u> week they <u>were</u> giving away a fantastic make-up bag. <u>She</u> <u>said</u> the only bad thing about it <u>was</u> the price. It <u>cost</u> 2 pounds fifty, which <u>Lily</u> <u>thought</u> <u>was</u> quite expensive.
Amy <u>said</u> <u>(thought)</u> "Glory" <u>sounded</u> like a really good magazine and <u>asked</u> if <u>she</u> <u>could</u> have a look at one of <u>hers</u>.
So Lily <u>told</u> <u>her</u> <u>to come</u> round to <u>her</u> house <u>that</u> afternoon and <u>she</u> <u>would</u> lend <u>her</u> the magazine from the week <u>before</u>. But <u>she</u> <u>asked</u> <u>her</u> <u>not to come</u> before 4 o'clock because <u>she</u> <u>wouldn't</u> be home until then.

S. 102 Übung 12

1. Ben said that he **would meet** Kate outside the cinema that evening.
2. The teacher told the children that they **could start** their homework as soon as they **had finished** exercise 2.
3. Holly asked me what I **was looking for**.
4. The man asked me what I **wanted**.
5. Sophie said that she **was** hungry because she **hadn't eaten** anything since breakfast.
6. Ben said that he **hadn't slept** well because he **had been** cold in the night.
7. Amy said that she **didn't know** what I **was talking about**.
8. Jack said that he **couldn't go** to school this week because he **was** ill.
9. Jack said that he **hadn't been able to go** to school last week because he **had been** ill.

Das Passiv

S. 105 Übung 1

2. they **are taught**
3. I **was paid**
4. they **were built**
5. he **has been caught**
6. we **hadn't been asked**
7. she **will be invited**
8. they **would have stolen**
9. I **would have been sent**
10. it **is kept**
11. they **are flown**
12. they **are going to be sold**

Das Passiv

Übung 2

A lot of building work **is being done** in the town at the moment. A new town centre **is being developed** and new office blocks and car parks **are being built**. A new school **is** also **being planned**.

Übung 3

When I got home yesterday, a lot of work **was being done** on the house. A new carpet **was being laid** on the stairs, a new kitchen **was being installed**, the living room walls **were being painted** and new curtains **were being put up** in my bedroom.

Übung 4

1 School uniform **must be worn** during school hours.
2 Hair **should be kept** off the face.
3 Small ear-rings **may be worn** by girls, but not by boys.
4 If possible, children **shouldn't be driven** to school.
5 Bicycles **can be left** in the stands provided.
6 Mobile phones **may be brought** to school but they **mustn't be used** in the classroom.
7 Classrooms **must be tidied** at the end of each school day.
8 No ball games **may be played** inside the school buildings.
9 Pupils who break the rules **may be suspended** and in serious cases **might even be expelled**.

Übung 5

Why do so many young people want **to become** celebrities? Ask them and you will hear all the usual reasons: They would like **to be paid** well for doing very little work, **to be invited** to glamourous parties, **to be upgraded** on planes and not least of all **to be admired** everywhere they go. Being a celebrity seems **to be** such an exciting life. Of course, life is only like that for the very few, but can you expect young people **to believe** that?

Übung 6

1 Have you seen this photo? It **was taken** at Dan's party but I don't know who **took** it.
2 **Did Germany win** the World Cup in 2006? – No, they **were beaten** in the semi-finals by Italy.

Lösungen

3   The older children **usually walk** to school but their baby brother **is always driven** to kindergarten.
4   **Has your neighbours' house been sold** yet? – No, they **have been trying** to sell it for about six months now so it's probably too expensive.
5   Why **were you born** in South Africa? – Because my parents **were living** there at the time.
6   We **couldn't use** the bathroom yesterday because a new shower **was being installed**.
7   When Mum came home, she **got** a lovely surprise. The living room **had been tidied**, the meal **had been cooked** and the table **had been laid**.
8   If you **leave** your bike here, it **may be stolen**.
9   If you **were offered** a lot of money to appear on a reality TV show and to make a fool of yourself, **would you do** it?
10 We **would have been able to** swim in the lake last summer if it **hadn't been polluted** by the new factory.
11 Do you believe celebs when they tell you they don't want **to be recognized**?

S. 110 Übung 7

1   The safari park is visited by thousands of people each year.
    It's popular because the animals aren't kept in cages there.
2   The book is being turned into a film,
    but the film isn't being released until next year.
3   The judges of a talent show were impressed by an eleven-year-old singer.
    But in the end the competition wasn't won by the little girl.
4   A concert was being given by the band to raise money for charity.
    But the event wasn't being organised by them.
5   A new football stadium has just been built in our town,
    but it hasn't been opened yet.
6   A window had been broken by the burglars,
    but the noise hadn't woken the neighbours.
7   50 people will be invited by the Casting Director to audition for a role in a daily soap.
8   The applicants won't be told immediately if they have got the part.
9   The story is going to be published in tomorrow's newspaper,
    but it isn't going to be printed on the front page.

Das Passiv

Übung 8

1. <u>She</u> will be told what to do.
2. <u>I</u> am being met by my grandparents at the airport.
3. Were <u>they</u> shown around New York by a guide?
4. <u>We</u> weren't driven to school this morning.

Übung 9

2. Jenny's flat <u>was broken into</u> last week.
3. A notice <u>has been put up</u> on the board.
4. The old houses <u>are going to be pulled down</u>.
5. The children <u>are looked after</u> by a nanny.
6. The baby <u>wasn't woken up</u> by the noise.
7. His mind <u>has been made up</u>.
8. The worksheets <u>will be handed out</u> at the beginning of the lesson by the teacher.
9. The lights <u>hadn't been switched off</u>.
10. Why <u>wasn't</u> a doctor <u>sent for</u> if the boy was so ill?

Übung 10

1. <u>No</u> questions will be asked.
2. <u>Nobody</u> has been seen in his shop for weeks.
3. <u>Nobody</u> was <u>ever</u> invited to their house.
4. <u>No</u> information was given to the press.
5. I want to know why <u>nothing</u> is being done about the pollution in this town.

Übung 11

1. The birthday card must be sent today.
2. A rabbit can be kept in the house or in the garden.
3. He ought to be told the truth.
4. The sandwiches can't be made the day before the party.
5. Must Kate's parents be told about the party?
8. I think the police should be called.
9. Nothing can be done to help him.

Übung 12

1. Are you taught how to cook at your school?
2. Is the event being organized by the record company?

Lösungen

3 Were they taken on a sightseeing tour of London?
4 Why isn't the new hospital going to be built?
5 Did your parents have to be told about the fire?
6 Were all the cakes sold at the fete?
7 Were the children being looked after?
8 When is the new road going to be opened?
9 Had your car been parked in a no-parking zone?
10 How often have you been told not to leave your shoes in front of the door?
11 Who was the song written by?

S. 117 Übung 13

1 Nowadays a lot of films are made in Vancouver.
2 The competition isn't being held this year.
3 The operation can't be done until next year.
4 The computers on the second floor weren't being used.
5 Your homework must be handed in before 9 am.
6 You won't be laughed at if you make a silly mistake.
7 The toys haven't been put away, they have been left on the floor.
8 You will be shown where to go.
9 It was only a small fire. The fire brigade didn't have to be called.
10 The oil had been checked and the tyres had been pumped up.

S. 118 Übung 14

1 English is spoken in most countries.
2 A new shower is being installed.
3 The money was found in his apartment (flat).
4 Every morning we are woken by the dog.
5 The girl had to be taken to hospital immediately. (… had to be rushed to hospital.)
6 Do you know when America was discovered?
7 The information will be sent by post tomorrow.
8 The books can be ordered on the Internet.
9 Where were these photos taken?
10 When must the dog be fed? (When does the dog have to be fed?)
11 Why did Tom have to be invited?
12 How often has he been told to close the window before he goes out?
13 I don't want to be recognized.

Nomen/*nouns*

Übung 1

2 This **box** is too small. Aren't there any larger ones? – Look in the attic. You'll find some larger **boxes** there.
3 Ben's got so many **books** but nowhere to put them. He really needs a few more **shelves** in his room.
4 Mum usually buys our **potatoes**, **tomatoes** and **eggs** from the market.
5 Who took those **photos** of me? They're terrible.
6 There were only three **people (BrE)/persons (AmE)** on the bus: two **women** and a small **child**.
7 Don't ask Jack to help you. He's got two left **hands** and two left **feet**.
8 An argument essay is an essay in which you have to discuss the **pros and cons** of a particular subject.
9 Have you got a dishwasher or do you have to wash the **dishes** yourself?
10 **Teenagers** often dream of becoming **celebrities** because they think that they must lead such glamourous **lives**.

Übung 2

2 Amy has brown eyes and beautiful long dark **hair**.
3 Sophie thinks she knows who stole her purse, but she has no **proof**.
4 Have you seen these brochures? They have some very useful **information** on how to help the environment.
5 **The homework was** too difficult. None of the children could do **it**.
6 I'm afraid **the news is** not good. Are you sure that you want to hear **it**?
7 I didn't like their new **furniture**. **It was** very uncomfortable.

Übung 3

1 Amy wanted to wear her new **trousers** to the party, but she couldn't find **them**. **They were** under her bed.
2 Do you know where **my glasses are**? – Yes, I saw **them** on the kitchen table a moment ago.
3 **The stairs were** very dirty. **They** hadn't been cleaned for a long time.
4 Somebody has called the police. **They are coming. They will** be here in a minute.
5 **These scissors are** no good. **They aren't** sharp enough.
6 Kate hadn't put her washing into the basket. **Her dirty clothes were lying** on her bedroom floor.
7 I like **your new trousers. They look** good.

Lösungen

Übung 4 (S. 124)

2. I'm looking for **some scissors**.
   I'm looking for **a pair of scissors**.
   There are **two pairs of scissors** in the drawer.
3. I need **some new pyjamas**.
   I need **a new pair of pyjamas**.
4. I have **some interesting news** for you.
   I have **an interesting piece of news** for you.

Übung 5 (S. 125)

1. The chairs were all broken, so we had to buy **some new ones**.
2. The train had left, so we had to wait for **the next one**.
3. Which T-shirt do you like better? **The red one or the yellow one**?
4. Those trousers don't look very nice. Why don't you buy **some new ones**.

Übung 6 (S. 126)

1. Uncle Jim is **my father's brother**.
2. **The winner of the competition** will receive 100,000 euros.
3. Ben isn't here at the moment. He's **at the doctor's**.
4. Have you read **today's newspaper**?
5. All the actors performed well but **the star of the show** was an eleven-year-old girl.
6. The Native Americans had already been living in the country for **thousands of years** before the white man came.
7. There were **hundreds of people** on the beach.
8. You will find **a list of the irregular verbs on the last page of your English book**.
9. Do you know **the names of Charles's sons/Charles' sons**?
10. The Statue of Liberty is **one of New York's most popular tourist attractions**.

Der bestimmte und der unbestimmte Artikel

Übung 1 (S. 129)

1. The ~~Life~~/life of a pop star isn't always glamourous.
2. — History/~~history~~ is not Dan's favourite subject. The only history he is interested in is **the** history of rock music.

Der bestimmte und der unbestimmte Artikel

3 **The** ~~Immigrants~~/immigrants who arrived in America between 1820 and 1920 came mainly from Europe.
4 — Immigrants/~~immigrants~~ are people who have left their home countries and now live in a different country.
5 Do you like — Indian food? **The** ~~Curries~~/curries they serve at the new Indian restaurant are delicious.
6 Mrs Davis enjoys working with children. **The** ~~Children~~/children she works with are all very well-behaved.

Übung 2 — S. 129

1 **Life on the reservations is very hard.**
2 **The Native Americans who live there often have no work.**
3 **Tourism is an important industry for them.**
4 **Some people think that tourist attractions like the Grand Canyon Skywalk will destroy the natural landscape.**

Übung 3 — S. 130

1 All children should drink — milk.
2 **The** ~~Milk~~/milk that is in the fridge is already sour.
3 For — breakfast Tom had a bowl of cornflakes and two pieces of toast.
4 **The** ~~Fish~~/fish we buy from the market is always very fresh.
5 **The** ~~Food~~/food at the restaurant was badly cooked and it was cold.

Übung 4 — S. 130

1 **For breakfast I ate a piece of toast.**
2 **I'll call you after lunch.**
3 **The lunch that Anna cooked for us was delicious.**

Übung 5 — S. 131

1 — Lake/~~lake~~ Constance is the English name for the *Bodensee*.
2 **The** Colorado River has been winding ist way through the Grand Canyon for millions of years.
3 — Mount/~~mount~~ McKinley is the highest mountain in **the** USA.
4 Where is the best snow for skiing? In **the** Alps or in **the** Rocky Mountains?
5 Dutch is the language that people speak in **the** Netherlands.

Lösungen

S. 131 Übung 6

1. Mount Everest is the highest mountain in the world.
2. Do you know how long the Colorado River is?
3. Lars has been to England twice but he has never been to the USA.

S. 132 Übung 7

1. Broadway
2. Ellis Island
3. <u>the</u> Big Apple
4. Manhattan
5. Chinatown
6. downtown
7. <u>the</u> Statue of Liberty
8. Ground Zero
9. Fifth Avenue
10. <u>the</u> Empire State Building
11. Central Park
12. <u>the</u> Brooklyn Bridge

S. 133 Übung 8

1. Amy is in — hospital. She's in **the** hospital in King's Road.
2. Ben's parents go to — church every Sunday. **The** ~~Church~~/church they go to is 800 years old.
3. Jack is in — prison. His father can't visit him because **the** prison he is in is too far away.
4. Amy usually goes to school by — bike or by — train, but sometimes her mother takes her in **the** car.

S. 133 Übung 9

1. Kate's brother is in hospital.
2. We are going to the airport by train.
3. The school (that) Amy goes to has more than 800 pupils/students.

S. 134 Übung 10

1. Today **most** children have TVs in their bedroom.
2. **Most of the** children in Tom's class have TVs in their bedroom.

Der bestimmte und der unbestimmte Artikel

3 I didn't know everybody at the party but I knew **most of the** people.
4 Tom has already read **most of the** Harry Potter books.
5 She had **the most** beautiful eyes I had ever seen, one was blue and two were green.

Übung 11

1 **Most children enjoy swimming.**
2 **Most of the children in our class live near the school.**
3 **Most of the jobs in the town are in tourism.**

Übung 12

1 Kate's father is an engineer and her mother is **a teacher**.
2 The school is quite large. It has almost **a thousand** students.
3 If you say that a restaurant is open 24/7, you mean that it is open 24 hours **a day**, seven days **a week**.
4 The school orchestra gives a concert twice **a year**, one is in December and the other is in June.
5 How many pence are there in a pound? – **A hundred**.
6 How much do the tomatoes cost? – Two pounds **a kilo**.

Übung 13

1 **How much pocket money do you get a month? – 50 euros.**
2 **How long have you been waiting? – For half an hour!**
3 **Tom: "How much does the hotel cost?"**
  David: "A hundred dollars a night."
  Tom: "A hundred dollars? That is too much."

Übung 14

2 Do we need anything from the shops? – Yes, a loaf of bread and **half a pound** of butter.
3 When does the film start? – In about **half an hour**.
4 I don't like Ben. I think he's **such an idiot**.
5 It took **quite a long time** but in the end we managed to install the new software.
6 Please don't make **such a noise**, I'm trying to concentrate.
7 Is it far from here to the station? – No, not really. It's only about **half a mile**.
8 Did you enjoy the film? – Yes, it had **quite an amusing ending**.
9 Jack, your room is in **such a mess**. Please tidy it now.

Lösungen

Übung 15 (S. 137)

1 I'm going shopping. Do you need anything? – Yes, half a pound of butter.
2 Don't make such a noise!
3 Sophie told me quite a funny joke yesterday.

Notwendige und nicht notwendige Relativsätze

Übung 1 (S. 138)

1 Blogging is a leisure pursuit **which/that** is becoming more and more popular.
2 Weblogs, or blogs for short, are diaries **which/that** people write online.
3 For those **who** enjoy sharing their feelings with the world, the Internet is a great place to be.
4 The problem is that the Internet is also a place **where** many people feel anonymous.
5 Not everything **that** people write online is acceptable.
6 Sometimes the things **which/that** they blog about can be very hurtful to others.
7 That is why some people's websites **whose** blogs are too personal are often shut down, and rightly so.

Übung 2 (S. 139)

2 It's about a young girl whose parents have died.
3 She's a brave girl who isn't easily frightened.
4 The people ~~who~~ she lives with are not always kind to her.
5 Nothing ~~that~~ she does is ever good enough for them.
6 Her bedroom is a small room ~~which~~ she has to share with three other children.

Übung 3 (S. 140)

2 The **bed I slept in was very comfortable.**
3 The **park rangers I spoke to were all very friendly.**
4 The **excursions we went on were fantastic fun.**
5 The **tress I took photos of were about four thousand years old.**
6 The **people I made friends with are going to visit me next summer.**

Übung 4 (S. 141)

1 The team who beat us in the semi-finals went on to win the tournament.
2 Gordon High, who beat us in the semi-finals, went on to win the tournament.
3 The tournament was held at the new stadium, which was built last year.

Notwendige und nicht notwendige Relativsätze

4   Each year it is an event which is very popular.
5   Ben, who scored the winning goal, is only 15 years old.
6   The boy who scored the winning goal is only 15 years old.
7   Ben's father, who was a famous footballer himself, was at the match to support him.
8   The man in the stands who kept jumping up and down was Ben's father.
9   The woman who was sitting next to him was his mother.
10 Ben, whose mother was a tennis star, is also an excellent tennis player.

Übung 5
S. 142

1a **None of the students had finished the exercise and they all had to do it for homework.**
1b **Only the students who hadn't finished the exercise had to do it for homework.**
2a **Tom has more than one sister, but the sister who emigrated to the USA now lives in Los Angeles.**
2b **Tom only has one sister. She emigrated to the USA and now lives in Los Angeles.**
3a **Only the clothes which were on the floor were dirty.**
3b **All the clothes were dirty and they were all on the floor.**

Übung 6
S. 143

The Native Americans

1   The first people to arrive in America came from Asia about 20,000 years ago. They were people— **who** moved from place to place in search of food.
2   They crossed the Bering Sound, **which** at that time formed a land bridge between the two continents of Asia and America.
3   The European settlers, **who** began arriving in the 1600s, called these people Indians because the first people— **who** had sailed from Europe to America— thought that they had arrived in India.
4   At first the Indians, **who** were mostly peaceful people, welcomed the new settlers and even helped them to survive.
5   But conflicts between them arose soon when the Europeans began to take land for themselves, **which** the Indians believed belonged to everyone.
6   The land was very important for the Indians, **whose** lives were close to nature, but the Europeans could not understand this.
7   They believed that land— **which** hadn't been fenced in— didn't belong to anyone.

Lösungen

8 To solve the problem, the American government decided to move all the Indian tribes— **who** were living in the Southwest— to the west of the Mississippi river, **where** they would be given new land. The journey was long and hard and many of the Cherokee Indians died on the way. Those— **who** survived— called it "The Trail of Tears".

9 After 1848, more and more white Americans— **who** were hoping to find gold in California— crossed the Mississippi into Indian territory.

10 Wars broke out and thousands of Indians were killed. By 1900 those— **who** were left— were forced to live on reservations.

11 As one Indian chief put it: "The white man made many promises to the Indians, but there was only one promise— ~~which~~ he kept: the one to take our land."

12 Life on the reservations, **where** there were few jobs, was hard and many of the Indians became alcoholics or died of white man's diseases.

13 Today the Indians, **who** are now known as Native Americans, no longer have to live on reservations. They can live in any city— ~~which~~ they wish to.

14 There are many of them— **who** have managed to lead successful lives. Some have become teachers, doctors or lawyers, and there are others— **who** have even become the bosses of billion-dollar businesses.

S. 145 Übung 7

The Skywalk

1 The Skywalk, **which** was opened in March 2007, is the Grand Canyon's latest attraction.

2 The views— ~~which~~ you get from the horseshoe-shaped glass observation platform of the Canyon 4,000 feet below— are awesome.

3 With this project the Hualapai Indians, **who** own the site, are hoping to tackle the problems of high unemployment on their reservation.

4 They feel that this is an investment which will bring them the money— ~~which~~ they desperately need.

5 But there are some people— **who** are not so happy about this new tourist attraction.

6 They are afraid that the highway— ~~which~~ the tribe plans to build in order to attract more visitors— will destroy the natural beauty of the land.

Adjektive und Adverbien

Übung 8

S. 146

The Mayflower Compact
1 In 1620 the Mayflower set sail from Plymouth in Britain for Virginia – a colony— **which** had been founded in the New World by British settlers in 1607.
2 On board were 35 Puritans – a religious group— **who** had not been allowed to practise their religion freely in Britain— – as well as a number of other passengers— **who** wanted to leave Britain for different reasons.
3 The voyage**,** **which** took 66 days, was long and hard.
4 When they finally reached the New World, they didn't land in Virginia, but further north at a place— **where** few Europeans had been before.
5 They called their new home Plymouth after the port— ~~which~~ they had sailed from in Britain.
6 Before landing, the Puritans wrote down a set of rules— ~~which~~ everybody had to agree to follow.
7 This Agreement**,** **which** later became known as The Mayflower Compact**,** was the beginning of democracy in America.

Übung 9

S. 146

1 **Kate, who was dancing with William, looked very happy.**
2 **Ben threw the ball to Jack, who then threw it to me.**
3 **Jack, whose parents split up before he was born, lives with his mother.**
4 **The bus (which/that) I was travelling on was almost empty.**
5 **I know a good restaurant where we can have lunch.**
6 **"The Mayflower", where we had lunch yesterday, serves very good food.**
7 **Do you know the German family who/that live in that house?**
8 **Did you find the sunglasses (which/that) you were looking for?**

Adjektive und Adverbien

Übung 1

S. 148

1 Horse riding is a **popular** sport in the UK.
2 Over 4 million people go riding **regularly**.
3 It can be a **thrilling** experience, but only if you do it **safely**.
4 You should wear a riding hat, boots and clothing that lets you move **freely**.
5 Riding is an **expensive** hobby, so before you buy all the equipment, you should make sure that it is the **right** one for you.

Lösungen

S. 149 Übung 2

1 Horses are **powerful** animals, so it is quite **natural** for you to feel a little **nervous/scared** at first.
2 But remember that a horse can sense immediately if its rider is **nervous/scared**.
3 So you must show him who is in control. But never get **angry**. Just try to stay as **calm** and **relaxed** as you can.

S. 150 Übung 3

1 Exeter is a town with a **growing** population.
2 Do you know who that rather **strange-looking** man is?
3 The **handpainted** vases were magnificent.
4 Yesterday I heard a very **amusing** story.
5 The house was at the end of a beautiful **tree-lined** avenue.
6 The whole world was **shocked** by Princess Diana's sudden and **unexpected** death in 1997.

S. 150 Übung 4

2 Sophie cut her foot on some **broken** glass.
3 Nobody was killed in the explosion but a lot of people were injured by **flying** glass.
4 The film had a **surprising** ending.
5 Yesterday police raided a factory in Old Road and recovered a number of **stolen** cars.
6 The **frightened** girl hid under the bed.
7 Toby is a talented actor with an **exciting** future ahead of him.
8 I don't know if I want to see the film. It has been given very **mixed** reviews.
9 Kate was most **disappointed** when she wasn't offered the job as a model.
10 The bank robber rushed out of the bank and jumped into a **waiting** car.

S. 151 Übung 5

2 **Tom asked a <u>very interesting</u> question.**
3 **The teacher advised the pupils not to read <u>badly-written books</u>.**
4 **Jack told me an <u>amusing story</u>.**

Adjektive und Adverbien

Übung 6 S. 152

1 The bus **usually** runs — on time.
2 **Always** Read/read — the instructions before you do the exercise.
3 Ben — isn't **often** at home in the evenings.
4 Emily **never** listens — in class.
5 Jane — doesn't **always** do her homework.
6 We **sometimes** visit — our grandparents at the weekends.
7 It — doesn't **often** snow in the winter.
8 Tim and Amy — aren't **usually** late for school.
9 We **hardly ever** go — to bed before 10 pm.
10 Ben — has **always** had to work hard.

Übung 7 S. 153

2 Ben and Sophie danced ⬇ around the room. (slowly) (*Verb + Adverb*)
3 The children spoke English ⬇. (well) (*Verb + Objekt + Adverb*)
4 Amy closed the door ⬇. (quietly) (*Verb + Objekt + Adverb*)
5 Dad drove the car ⬇ into the garage. (carefully) (*Verb + Objekt + Adverb*)
6 Tom ⬇ agreed to help Jack in the test. (stupidly) (*Adverb + Verb + langes Objekt*)
7 Ben ⬇ read the letter that was lying on the table. (quickly) (*Adverb + Verb + langes Objekt*)
8 Jack's daughters always work ⬇ for school. (hard) (*Verb + Adverb*)
9 The children played their music ⬇. (loudly) (*Verb + Objekt + Adverb*)
10 Tom behaved ⬇ at the family party. (badly) (*Verb + Adverb*)
11 The home crowd cheered ⬇ when their team scored the winning goal. (happily) (*Verb + Adverb*)
12 The teacher ⬇ explained the rules for indirect speech to the children. (patiently) (*Adverb + Verb + langes Objekt*)

Übung 8 S. 154

1 Last night **we went to bed early.**
2 They **are going to the concert on Friday.**
3 **What time did you get to school this morning?**
4 **I'll meet you outside the school gates at 2 pm.**
5 **Tim has invited us to his party on Saturday.**
6 **There were a lot of people on the beach at the weekend.**

Lösungen

Übung 9 (S. 155)

2 We ⬇ go to the cinema at the weekends. (often)
3 Sophie did her homework in her bedroom ⬇. (after lunch)
4 The hockey team won the match ⬇. (easily)
5 Kate sang ⬇ at the concert on Friday. (beautifully)
6 ⬇ be polite to your teachers. (always)
7 I have ⬇ been to the USA. (never)
8 Sophie ⬇ has to help her mother at home. (often)
9 He can ⬇ remember names ⬇. (1 never, 2 well)
10 They ⬇ speak English ⬇. (1 hardly ever, 2 at home)

MANZ LERNHILFEN

MANZ – wenn's ernst wird!

Durch gezieltes Training zu besseren Noten!

ISBN 978-3-7863-1062-4

ISBN 978-3-7863-2028-9

ISBN 978-3-7863-3029-5

Wir bieten Lernhilfen für die Fächer Deutsch, Englisch, Französisch, Latein, Mathematik, Physik und Biologie.

- Jahrgangsbände mit dem Stoff des ganzen Schuljahrs für diejenigen, die generell Schwierigkeiten in einem Fach haben
- Schuljahrsübergreifende Themenbände für Schüler, die sich mit bestimmten Inhalten schwertun
- Sämtliche Lernhilfen mit zahlreichen und vielfältigen Übungen
- Alle Übungsbände mit ausführlichen Musterlösungen
- Außerdem im Programm: Bücher zur Vorbereitung auf den Haupt- und Realschulabschluss sowie auf diverse andere Prüfungen

Weitere Informationen über das MANZ Lernhilfen-Programm erhalten Sie in Ihrer Buchhandlung oder auf unserer Internetseite www.manz-verlag.de

MANZ LERNHILFEN

Einfach besser in der Schule werden!

Mit dem notwendigen Grundwissen Schritt für Schritt zum Klassenziel!

ISBN 978-3-7863-3203-9

ISBN 978-3-7863-2441-6

ISBN 978-3-7863-2203-0

- Alles auf einen Blick: Übersichtliche Lerneinheiten mit Wiederholung – Beispiel – Übungen auf je einer Doppelseite
- Kleinschrittiges Vorgehen für besseres Verständnis
- Ausführliche Musterlösungen zur Kontrolle
- Tests mit Notenschlüssel zur Selbstbewertung
- Orientiert an den Lehrplänen für 8-jährige Gymnasien
- Gerade auch für schwächere Schüler geeignet

Einfach besser – die Lernhilfenreihe für Deutsch, Englisch, Französisch und Mathe in der Sekundarstufe I

Weitere Informationen über das MANZ Lernhilfen-Programm erhalten Sie in Ihrer Buchhandlung oder auf unserer Internetseite www.manz-verlag.de